Advance praise for

Coaching CLUES

"A virtual coach for everyone who wishes to enhance their effectiveness in working with clients, *Coaching* CLUES offers deep wisdom from one who is herself a true master. This is a 'must have' addition to your library."
Richard Whiteley, author of *The Customer-Driven Company* and *The Corporate Shaman*

"Very compelling—I found myself wanting to get to the end of the stories to see how things turned out! Marian's humor is very effective as is her ability to model how a good coach supports others. *Coaching* CLUES will make a real contribution to the field with its practical and creative suggestions that OD professionals can use in their work."
Anna Marie Valerio, Organization Leadership Consultant, IBM

"*Coaching* CLUES takes coaching and brings it to reality. These stories reflect the fact that people can change, if they want to change, and if they have the right guidance in doing so… I am confident that *Coaching* CLUES will appeal to executives as well as coaches."
Helaine Suval, Senior Vice-President and General Merchandise Manager, macys.com

"With remarkable insight, Marian transforms theory to practice and concepts become realities as she paints a picture of possibility that is hard to resist. In her hands even the ingrained cynic (I was one) is inspired to try new tools and embrace the daunting challenge of changing personal behaviors."
Peter Vincent, Senior Vice-President Human Resources, Occidental Oil and Gas Corporation

"Psychological therapy will probably improve your personal life but if you think you don't need coaching to improve in your professional life, think again. Marian's incredible insight and her years of experience and observation—which she has packed into this book—has given me the confidence and weapons I've needed to face the ever more demanding workplace environment. *Coaching* CLUES, with its powerful tool kit, should be on everyone's list of must-reads."
Virginia Pagetti, Vice-President, Global Marketing, Avon Products Inc.

Coaching
CLUES

The business agenda at the start of the twenty-first century focuses on working with change and developing people's potential and performance. The *People Skills for Professionals* series brings this leading theme to life with a practical range of personal development and human resource guides for anyone who wants to get the best from their people.

Other titles in the Series

COACHING FOR PERFORMANCE
GROWing People, Performance and Purpose
Third edition
John Whitmore

INNER LEADERSHIP
Realize Your Self-leading Potential
Simon Smith

LEADING YOUR TEAM
How to Involve and Inspire Teams
Second edition
Andrew Leigh and Michael Maynard

MANAGING TRANSITIONS
Making the Most of Change
William Bridges

MEDIATION FOR MANAGERS
Resolving Conflict and Rebuilding
Relationships at Work
John Crawley and Katherine Graham

NLP AT WORK
The difference that makes a difference
in business
Second edition
Sue Knight

POSITIVE MANAGEMENT
Assertiveness for Managers
Paddy O'Brien

THE POWER OF INFLUENCE
Tom E. Lambert

THE TRUST EFFECT
Creating the High Trust,
High Performance Organization
Larry Reynolds

Coaching
CLUES

Real Stories, Powerful Solutions, Practical Tools

Marian J. Thier

NICHOLAS BREALEY
PUBLISHING

LONDON
YARMOUTH, MAINE

First published by
Nicholas Brealey Publishing in 2003

3–5 Spafield Street
Clerkenwell, London
EC1R 4QB, UK
Tel: +44 (0)20 7239 0360
Fax: +44 (0)20 7239 0370

PO Box 700
Yarmouth
Maine 04096, USA
Tel: (888) BREALEY
Fax: (207) 846 5181

http://www.nbrealey-books.com
http://www.coachingclues.com

ISBN 1-85788-337-3

British Library Cataloguing in Publication Data
A catalogue record for this book is available from the British Library.

Printed in Finland by WS Bookwell.

To my trusted and loving coaches:
daughter Whitney Thier, her husband Mark Gillespie and their children
Dalton Jane and Charles Eden Gillespie;
sons Antony and J Alexander Thier and his wife, Tamara Gould

Contents

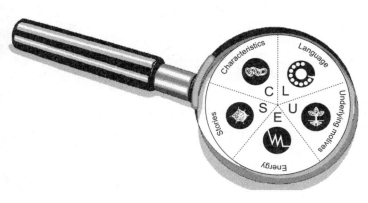

Energy   75

Stories   95

All CLUES Categories   123

**PART II: THE TOOLKIT—A USER'S GUIDE FOR APPLYING
THE FIVE COACHING CLUES** 133

Acknowledgments

I am blessed with a life of good fortune and I am grateful for it. My brother, Hon. Arnold C. Rapoport, is unfailingly in support of me. My assistant Julie Heins is incredibly able and thoughtful. Pamela Joseph's friendship and belief in the project propelled me forward. This team helped bring the book to reality: Maggie Lichtenberg, Jayn Stewart, Chris Kochansky, Regula Noetzl, and the reading group. Nicholas Brealey the collaborative publisher dispels any notion of a difficult working relationship.

Of course, tremendous respect and appreciation go to colleagues and the many folks I have coached. Your commitment to making a difference in your worlds and partnership for growth create lives of purpose.

Introduction: About Coaching

*T*he new profession of coaching—working with individuals and small groups to improve their social skills and effectiveness in the workplace—has evolved out of the field of management consulting over the past two decades, and my professional life has evolved along with it.

As happened with many of us in the beginning, my coaching career began by request rather than by design. In the late 1980s I was brought into a large manufacturing company by the Forum Corporation to work with senior executives on a new leadership initiative. Part of the plan for this process was what's called a 360° feedback report: Each executive would be evaluated by people who worked with them at their own level and by those "higher" and "lower" in the corporate structure. Each would also be provided with assistance in interpreting the resulting reports and developing action plans to address problems and performance gaps.

For most of the feedback recipients, this was the first time they had ever gotten unfiltered data from their constituents, the people they worked with directly. They wanted to talk about the results. They wanted to know how their actions caused specific reactions in others, what could be done to alter those existing patterns of behavior that had negative effects, and how to assess the success of their efforts to make positive changes. It was my role to facilitate this inquiry.

Almost immediately people began to ask for additional time with me to help them improve their skills as individuals

and leaders. While I had no background in therapy, I did have a master's degree in adult development, some terrific colleagues with whom to talk over issues as they arose, and the resources of the New York City Public Library.

In addition, as part of an earlier project (the development of *Think Tank: The Game of Creative Problem Solving*® in 1985), I had sought out a primatologist at the Bronx Zoo to help me improve my observational skills. He taught me the importance of paying attention to small, subtle actions as well as larger, more obvious ones, because every example of behavior contributes to a deeper understanding of the individual or group that one is studying. He also warned me against extrapolating a universal truth from one set of behaviors and applying it to a different situation or individual.

It was significant to me that the primatologist recorded and reported what he saw in as factual and straightforward a way as possible. He postulated possible reasons for the behaviors he observed, but he did not judge them. It seemed to me that if I could do the same in the context of people working together within an organization, and then play back to those people what they said and did and ask if the behaviors matched their intentions, I could help them make change by choice, improve their skills, and gain more control over the results of their actions. I took the plunge and began working with the company's executives as a corporate coach.

For me, learning to be an effective coach has been like learning the art of cooking. Both require curiosity, willing teachers, coursework, experimentation, and a guiding purpose; both involve a journey from learning the basic principles and skills to creating one's own techniques and recipes. Dozens, maybe hundreds, of clients later, I take pride in being a pioneer and a veteran in this field.

Today, what used to be the purview of a few people who trained themselves to be coaches—and their privileged clients—is a growing industry, complete with coaching schools and professional associations. In 1999, for the first time, the worldwide International Coaches Federation began to offer credentials for coaches, and I was certified as a master coach.

Once in an interview I was asked to sum up what it is that makes an effective personal or team coach. Now that I've had some time to ponder the question, here are three key points to remember:

❑ A coach is not a business partner, therapist, buddy, or confidant. The coaching relationship is a negotiated partnership in which all parties must respect each other and remain committed to the boundaries of a professional relationship.

❑ Small changes can make a huge difference. Some of the people you will read about in this book take what might seem like very tiny steps. Together my clients and I consciously select one or two critical behaviors to change, those that have the potential for a wide impact. Also, it is crucial that both the coach and the client are willing to experiment with different ways to change a behavior. There is no silver bullet, no quick cure or magic formula that can alter a lifelong habit overnight.

❑ Authenticity is the coin of the realm. Many managers are so isolated and insulated, many team members so busy, that they lack the chance to talk to the people they work with in an unfiltered, honest way. I observe my clients in action, tell them what I see, and ask if that's what they're trying to achieve. I show them how others react to them. If what the mirror reflects is not their desired self, I provide tools to help them be more effective. In other words, I care enough for my clients that we can be truthful with one another.

With increasing frequency I receive requests from people who would like to observe me at work—to follow me into the kitchen while I cook, as it were. I explain that this isn't possible because it would violate the privacy that is an important aspect of my relationship with my clients. Nevertheless, I do have nearly 15 years' worth of knowledge and experience, and *Coaching* CLUES is designed to share some of what I have learned, including the model I have developed to ensure that as an observer of human interactions I can see the forest—the

whole person or team—as well as the trees, the specific actions and reactions of individuals.

This book is about people, not things. Although I'll begin with a description of the CLUES model and have arranged the stories that follow within that framework, its five elements aren't meant to be rigid or exclusive categories. Think of them instead as representing key dimensions of the interactions between individuals and within groups (listed in the Contents as "individual story" or "team story"). In Part I, the heart of *Coaching* CLUES, I'll use narrative to present eleven stories—to take you along with me as I meet a person or team, analyze their situation (read the clues), develop a coaching "tool" or technique to help, and assess the results. Part II describes twelve coaching tools that I've found especially useful over the years.

The stories are written in the first person and the present tense in hopes of keeping them "in the moment" and alive. The people in these stories "try on" new patterns of behavior that may conflict with old habits, which is both a brave thing to do and, for many, a strange experience. I have tried to capture the process of becoming aware of an old habit, trying an option to alter it, and gaining a new skill or set of skills. You will note that the results are positive in all the cases I've chosen to write about, even when the process was difficult. To me, there would be no purpose in showing an example that ended in failure. Although there is no ready-made, pat solution to every problem (that's what makes coaching such a creative and challenging profession), these "tools"— approaches and techniques—are among the most effective in my repertoire, and I want to give you, the reader, the confidence to try them for yourself.

You might use *Coaching* CLUES in a number of ways:

❑ Read it from end to end without any game plan or agenda, for an overview of management and work-life issues and techniques, and of the change process.
❑ Identify a skill or a tool that interests you (these are listed just below the titles at the beginning of each chapter) and concentrate on the story or stories that deal with it.

- ❑ Use the stories as case studies, reading the "situation" part only at first and then figuring out what you think is going on and what you would do to change it for the better.
- ❑ Apply the CLUES model to help you identify the most predominant factors in a given situation.
- ❑ Devise your own "tool" to address each situation and compare it with the one described in the book.
- ❑ Reflect on why the tools outlined in the book succeed, and what impact other approaches might have in similar situations.
- ❑ Use the tools as standalone aids to help you meet any challenges that you may be facing.

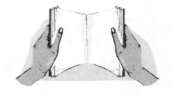

The settings and characters in this book are fictional, but they are based on real-life experience. If you see yourself, colleagues, or clients in the stories, don't be surprised. As human beings we all face similar challenges in life and work.

Whether you are a coach in training or an established practitioner looking to enlarge your repertoire, a newly promoted manager learning the ropes or a senior executive seeking to improve your managerial skills, a freelance worker or an entrepreneur, I hope you will find the ideas and information presented here interesting, thought-provoking, and, above all, useful.

1

The CLUES Model

Whether he or she is working with an individual or a group, a coach's ultimate goal is to help the client or clients solve problems that may be preventing them from achieving their full potential in the workplace—and perhaps in other arenas of life as well. The first step in this process is careful observation: What do people think the problem is and what are their own stated goals? What do they say about themselves and others? And, most importantly, how do they actually act and react in a given real-life situation?

The coach's first role, then, is that of an observer. But human interactions are endlessly complex. How can one filter out what is essentially extraneous and focus on those specific attitudes, habits, and behaviors that may be standing in the way of an individual's or group's success?

The CLUES model represents a method for organizing one's observations, a way of looking at behavior from five key points of view:

The CLUES model

- ❑ *Characteristics*: personal traits, preferences, and behavioral themes.
- ❑ *Language*: the implications of verbal, written, and bodily expression.
- ❑ *Underlying motives*: "drivers" that influence direction, choices, and action.
- ❑ *Energy*: factors that drain, nurture, or energize us.
- ❑ *Stories*: what a person talks about and what is said about him or her.

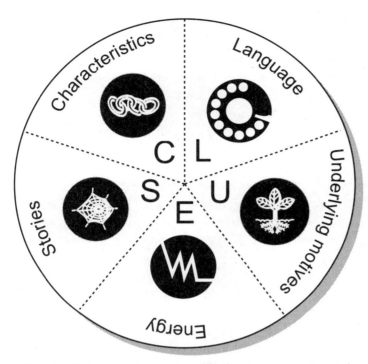

Naturally, all of these categories of behavior come into play in any given situation, but the CLUES framework can help us identify which are most important and which might point to the best avenue for change.

Before going on to our stories, let's take a closer look at examples of observations that fit into each of the CLUES categories—without, for now, speculating on any possible changes that a coach might advise or suggest.

Each person is unique in terms of his or her personal traits, preferences, and the behavioral themes revealed in specific actions. Patterns of characteristics, intended and unintended, may be seen in the strategies the individual uses to approach the world, and these patterns will certainly affect his or her contributions in the workplace.

When Company X suffered from the consequences of slow decision making in one of its departments, the following Characteristics clues led me to identify Tetsuko, a key employee in that department, as being overly cautious and afraid to take risks:

CHARACTERISTICS

Example

❏ Requests a lot of supporting facts and data when making decisions.
❏ Comes in early, stays late.
❏ Walls peppered with graphs and charts cutting the same information in different ways.
❏ Stacks of work on desk and floor.
❏ Asks others what they think and rarely offers her opinion.

LANGUAGE

How a person uses verbal, written, and body language will profoundly affect how others interpret his or her actions and intentions. The choice of words and terms, the structure of language, speech patterns, tone of voice, and the use of gesture combine to create an impression of what a person is like.

Example

Jake, a middle manager, comes across as a person who is uncomfortable with people in authority. The Language clues are:

❏ Highly verbal with peers and direct reports, but almost silent when in the presence of a person of higher rank.
❏ Uses short, clipped phrases with management and complex sentences with others.
❏ Doesn't make eye contact with the person in charge.
❏ Sits absolutely still in meetings with management—looks like he is trying to be invisible.

UNDERLYING MOTIVES

A person might say that he or she is working toward one set of goals when actually his or her actions are being influenced by something very different. Motivation almost always extends beyond what is evident or professed, and sometimes (but not always) this is relevant to a coaching situation.

Example

Franco is a hard-working engineer who tells his boss during a performance review that he wants to be a project manager. When Franco is queried about his plans, however, these Underlying motives clues indicate another agenda:

❏ Part-owner in family-run local business.
❏ Landlord of two rental units.
❏ Taking business classes with a marketing emphasis.

❑ Turned down relocation at previous company.
❑ Volunteers for locally based projects.

How, when, and to what degree a person is productive is a guide to his or her physical and mental output. Some people might be more productive at certain times of the day; some fare better working alone and others in teams; the office environment can drain or enliven workers; and what is stressful for one person can be enriching to another.

Susan is very much an extrovert who is effective and secure when working with others and awkward when given assignments to complete on her own. The Energy clues are:

❑ Pauses mid-morning to make lunch arrangements; eats at her desk if she has no companion, but never goes to the cafeteria alone.
❑ Is a member of several work teams at once.
❑ Often stays late and can be counted on to participate in sports leagues.
❑ When given an individual assignment, frequently asks others for input and advice—they all seem to know that she needs the contact, not the information.

What a person talks about and what is said about him or her are, of course, extremely valuable as clues in any situation. People's stories reveal what they think about, the highlights and pitfalls of their work history, who they have worked with well and poorly, and what motivates or discourages them.

Brian seems to have high potential as a leader within his company. The Stories clues about him are:

❑ Tells people when they first meet him that he knows the CEO (clever about the way he introduces the fact, embedded in a story about a pertinent topic).
❑ Tales are upbeat and optimistic.
❑ Asks questions about topics he knows, e.g., industry history and potential, emerging markets, golf and skiing, fine wines.
❑ Others regale you with stories of the good times they've had with Brian and the people he knows.

ENERGY

Example

STORIES

Example

Every situation can be mined for information from different CLUES categories. For example, in observing the man I have used as the model for the fictional Brian as he interacted with other people in the workplace, I found many Characteristics clues that fit the universal definition of an effective leader: He seemed people centered, business savvy, polite, and engaged. His behavior with regard to Language clues was very distinct: He stood upright, shook hands, and made friendly physical contact with people; he looked at the person talking and smiled often. He also used Energy to extend himself and rarely seemed tired or distracted. And whether these behaviors came naturally to him or had been learned, his Underlying motive was quite clear—Brian wanted to be a senior executive.

In the stories that follow, however, I will focus on the CLUES category that is most relevant to each. This narrowing down of the field—identifying one or two key aspects of behavior on which to focus—is the second step in successful coaching, the one that, as I hope these stories will show, enables a coach to reach into the "toolkit" (see Part II) to choose or devise the particular approach that will best suit specific clients and situations.

Part I

Real Stories and Powerful Solutions

Characteristics

2

Silence Is Not Golden

SKILL: Speaking up

TOOL: The index card system

CLUES CATEGORY: Characteristics

Some people are overwhelmed by the thought of speaking up in public, no matter how small the audience. Providing them with feedback that their reticence is unacceptable only makes matters worse, especially if they come from a culture or a family background that values quiet, behind-the-scenes contributions over self-assertion in a group setting.

In this story we observe someone who learns how to employ a simple device in order to modify her behavior until she is confident and experienced enough to "go it alone."

THE SITUATION

Mei Wong is referred to me by the director of diversity education of a large financial institution. He tells me that Mei is a senior IS (information systems) professional, regarded as a first-rate technician in the company, but that she does not speak up in meetings and this is becoming a problem.

In the course of our initial call the director says, "I know it's not uncommon for Asians to have a difficult time participating in open meetings, where a lot of ideas are kicked around and everyone's expected to put in their two cents' worth. So I'm sympathetic. On the other hand, Mei often represents her division at top-level meetings, and we need her input on the spot. We can't afford to have her be so silent."

THE APPROACH

I make an appointment to visit Mei in her office. (I doubt I would get very far with her over the phone, that's way too impersonal.)

I envision a slight and quiet woman. She is not quiet: I can hear her loud voice through the door while I'm waiting in the reception area. Her speech is staccato with lots of trills, almost like a musician practicing scales. And from my vantage point it sounds like she talks very fast.

Mei *is* slight, though, tiny in fact: under five feet tall and certainly under 100 pounds. Initially we talk about her academic background, her move to the United States, and her job history. It turns out that she was recruited by five global companies and chose this one because of its sizeable proportion of Asians at senior levels. When I ask if she thinks she's quiet in meetings, her reply is quick and affirmative. I follow with an inquiry about the impact of her quietness.

Mei answers with a question of her own: "Do you think they'll fire me because I don't talk in meetings? Are you a final warning?"

I tell Mei the truth as I know it (although companies sometimes have agendas that are not revealed to me).

When I ask Mei to return to my original question she's quite frank: "If my job would not be so critical to this company, I'm sure they would replace me. I listen well in meetings, but I am very uncomfortable to talk. Where I grew up it was considered very impolite to talk up in public."

We discuss the origin and results of that cultural norm. I wonder why she talks so easily (and loudly) in her office and on the phone. Mei explains that it's all right to speak out when asked, or in private. But putting yourself forward in a public setting is different.

I ask if she knows of any Asians who have learned to adapt to the more direct corporate culture of the West. Mei tells me about classes she attended to learn how to work in US companies. "They teach how to eat with knives and forks, order from menu, travel with colleagues, give presentations, and yes, attend meetings. I already took the class. I can eat fine, but I still hear my parents scold me for speaking out when I should be quiet. They told me that the duck with the loudest quack is easiest for the hunter to spot and kill." Many arguments to repudiate that statement come to mind, but I know they are powerless against the proverbs of her parents.

I ask Mei what's she's tried so far. She tells me about some attempts that have been self-punishing, on the whole, rather than reinforcing: no lunch, or stay an hour longer at work, or no TV if she does not say at least two things in a meeting.

Mei describes her meeting behavior: Come in at the last minute to avoid small talk, take notes, and listen. When the meeting is over she writes up her notes and condenses them into an email that she distributes immediately to those who attended the meeting.

Everyone appreciates those emails, she says; she knows this because people tell her so.

I read a couple of meeting-summary emails and realize what a crisp, clear writer Mei is. I suspect that half of the problem is that the meeting attendees would like to hear what Mei is thinking when they're together—it's frustrating for them to receive the benefit of her insights only after the fact. Since many of her colleagues have open, freewheeling, and productive discussions with her one-to-one, they can't comprehend why the setting makes such a huge difference.

I ask if anyone brings laptops to meetings. Mei says that's not allowed because executive meetings are supposed to be confidential. I wonder if I can get them to revisit that outdated notion, since it seems perfectly all right for Mei to summarize the meeting and distribute that summary by email afterward. However, that's a separate issue for the moment.

The next time we meet I bring index cards of different colors with me. I ask Mei which color looks like a question card to her. She picks the blue ones. Next comes the idea card—pink— and finally the opinion card—yellow.

THE APPLICATION

I explain the system to Mei. Whenever she attends a meeting, as she listens to the discussion she is to write down questions, ideas, or opinions as they surface: questions on blue cards, ideas on pink, and opinions on yellow.

Mei is concerned that she won't have time to take her usual notes because she'll be so busy writing on the cards. We discuss just what she thinks her role is in these meetings. During our conversation a light-bulb-going-on smile appears on her face. All at once, Mei says, she realizes that her note taking has been a substitute for participation.

What would it be like to attend a meeting and not take notes, Mei wonders aloud. "Who would summarize the meeting? What would I do during the meeting? I guess I'd listen and use the cards. What would people think of me changing my role? What if I don't have anything to write on the cards?" We agree that she'll experiment by attending the next meeting with only cards in hand instead of her customary notepad. I suggest that she forewarn people so they won't expect the usual email summary from her afterward.

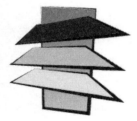

We rehearse—an important part of the process. I read Mei a case study from a magazine and ask her to fill in the cards as she listens. When we're done, I note that there are far more blue (questions) and pink (ideas) cards than yellow ones (opinions). Then I ask Mei to read aloud what she wrote on the cards. She complies smoothly, without a problem.

Mei wants to rehearse once more before going live. This time I ask her to read each card out loud as soon as she writes it. That way, I explain, her ideas will automatically be related to the subject at hand; she won't have to summarize the whole train of thought later. This is much harder for her because she has to interrupt me to interject her question, idea, or opinion.

We develop a rhythm: I read, Mei writes, and I naturally pause as I see her complete a card.

For both of us the hitch will be transitioning from Mei and Marian to Mei and a group. Mei herself comes up with the solution—she'll send an email.

To everyone who's expected at the next meeting she writes:

"Pat Yakima, the Director of Diversity Education, brought in a coach to help me participate more in meetings. As a result of our work, I am going to use a system of different color cards. I will write as you speak, then read my cards when they seem appropriate. I will appreciate your help. I will not send the usual meeting summary email."

THE RESULTS

"Marian, it was so funny at the meeting," Mei told me. "Everyone asked me to explain the system. I did and someone said that's the most he's ever heard me say in public. Then, during the meeting, they kept watching to see if I was writing. They didn't talk nearly as much as usual."

"Well," I say, in suspense, "did you read what you wrote?"

"I think you would not approve; but I made a pact with myself to read at least two cards. And I did achieve that."

"Great, Mei! Tell me about it."

"Well, at the beginning of the meeting I wrote only a couple of blue cards. Then Richard, from quality assurance, made a proposal that would involve IS. I wrote quite a few cards of all colors. Richard wanted to know if I was writing about his proposal. I picked up a yellow opinion card and read it to him. Everyone was looking at me, so I began to shake and couldn't say anything else. But Richard asked to take my cards to his department and made an appointment with me to talk about my thoughts right after the meeting."

"And how do you feel?"

Mei thinks a bit before responding. "It was definitely better than before. The system is a good idea because it gives me a way to speak out. But I still feel disobedient to my parents' training and that makes me shake."

As usual with people I coach, I assure her that it's acceptable to scrap the experiment if it isn't working.

"I think," she says, "I'm going to use the system when there's not so much pressure, until I stop shaking." Mei explains that she attends several small-group standing meetings with people she knows well. Although she is usually mostly quiet in this context as well, she feels comfortable enough to keep trying the color card method with them: "I'll quack along with everyone else."

I tell Mei that I think that's a great idea and we decide to stay in touch by phone.

For a while Mei and I talk once a week to discuss her progress. She uses the index card system in small-group settings and there's a noticeable difference in her level of participation. "I find the cards are useful to me after the meetings to help organize my thinking and planning. I bet you didn't think of that as a side benefit." She's teasing me a bit, but Mei's correct: Often tools developed for one purpose have other uses and unexpected side benefits.

I expected Mei would be able to shed the cards within three months, but in the end that took almost an entire birth cycle. At eight months she went into a large, high-level meeting cardless for the first time and afterward reported that she didn't shake at all.

Mei continues to struggle with some of the issues we addressed together. She informs me that people want to know why she stopped taking notes and sending her summary emails. "I tell them they can't have it both ways—either I speak up at meetings, using the card tool, or I sit in silence and take notes. Most people say it's more valuable to have me participate. I'd like to tell them to get someone else to take notes if they think it's so valuable. But that would be too confrontational for me."

For now, I say to myself.

3

Clutter, Clutter Everywhere and not a Spot to Think

SKILL: Organization

TOOL: Spring cleaning day

CLUES CATEGORIES: Characteristics, Energy, Stories

The physical environment in which people work reflects an organization's corporate culture, and what managers encourage (or discourage) in terms of dress, office decor, personalization of employee workspaces, etc., can have major consequences—both intended and unintended—for individual and collective productivity.

Here we meet a group of people who, in the service of stimulating creativity, have cultivated the art of clutter. In this case, though, it's beginning to get in the way of their effectiveness; at the same time, the free-spirited nature of the advertising agency where they work makes a conventional approach to organization unacceptable. What to do?

THE SITUATION

While walking around this ad agency where I've been hired to coach a team, I notice clutter everywhere. It's as though there's

a contest to see who can have the most overwhelming office—the most files, mementos, toys, pictures, and pending work. There's stuff all over the place.

One day when the team and I are meeting, I ask if they're ready for another of my quasi-official "observations." I've been watching them at work off and on for a few weeks, and periodically we've met all together so that I can share with them something I've noticed about the team or the organization: patterns of behavior that might seem simple or insignificant but might be having a significant impact on what they're doing. They seem to like these sessions. As someone said, "It's like 'Where's Waldo?'—Marian searches through the big picture to find a hidden piece."

Being careful not to sound like I'm a parent criticizing them for having messy rooms, I read off an inventory-like list of items in each office, hallway, and conference room. Here are some sample entries:

Jana's office:
27 photos—18 of the same dog
8 frames tarnished or chipped
photos on all surfaces, including desk, shelves, and table
2 bouquets of old, dried-up flowers in vases without water

David's office:
7 stacks of folders on shelves and floor
tallest stack, 15" high & leaning against other stacks
1 stack appears to have fallen, so papers are spread about
2 Power Bars in midst of piles of papers

Ling's office:
Folders neatly stacked on floor behind desk and in front of credenza
5 food containers under desk
stopped counting books at 100
1 bookshelf—holds about 1/3 of total books (the rest on floor)

Conference room A:
18 markers, 6 work, 12 dry
3 broken chairs
all flipcharts and whiteboards contain writing/drawing
9 inspirational posters on walls, 3 in cracked frames

Mailroom hallway:
11 empty boxes outside door
refuse container upside down
1 box of company stationery on floor
water cooler empty, 4 paper cups on floor
announcement board contains current messages and some from up to 3 months ago
announcement board cork torn

Then I ask for thoughts about the list. People laugh and make off-hand remarks: "Well, we're so busy we don't have time to straighten up." "We need more maintenance people." "Things just keep piling up." "I like to have my stuff around." Someone adds, somewhat inexplicably, "To the victor go the spoils."

I push a little. Doesn't all this—broken chairs, trash in public spaces, the outdated message board—interfere with the creative process? After a collective "Well…" they begin to vent about how the current state of disorganization and disrepair does cause problems: They can't find things; it's hard to get work done; it's depressing to see cracked picture frames that no one has time to fix; it makes people anxious to see unread and unsorted piles of paper that they haven't looked through.

Although they seem to agree that things are out of control, they all talk as though there's nothing they can do about it.

Now on familiar ground, I take another tack: "You must get some benefits from all the clutter. What are they?" The under-30s (the majority) say things like, "This is like my dorm room. I sort of feel like I haven't grown up yet and I like that." An older employee remarks, "There's a sense of having my intellectual property within reach. I want to be able to get at research, client engagements, and my notes without effort." Someone else chimes in, "Well, it's stimulating to see all these things. I get ideas from what's lying around. And I feel comforted by my photos."

"On a scale from one to ten," I ask, "how much value do you get from having the office the way it is?" They think about it, they discuss, they joke around a bit. Ultimately their response is clear. All too often the clutter is in the way.

THE APPROACH

Now I'm caught between two truisms: A messy desk is a sign of a messy mind, but creative people need stimuli to jumpstart the process. My intention is to help the agency develop a sufficient degree of organization for people to work more efficiently without making the place seem sterile and rule-bound. I also know that this team in particular won't have much use for a standard seminar on how to organize their workspaces (previously the agency had held a workshop on time management; it had been well attended but none of the consultant's recommendations had ever been implemented).

At my next meeting with this particular team, someone challenges me with, "What ever happened to your little campaign to help us get rid of our clutter? Did you give up on us—too far gone?"

"Actually," I retort, "I've got an idea. Let me run it by you." My idea is based on one of the organization's established corporate customs: During this era, while other white-collar companies had "dress-down days"—one day a week when employees could come into the office in casual clothes—at this ad agency most people wore casual clothes most of the time, but on Thursdays everyone came to work in suits or jackets and ties, or in pantsuits or dresses.

"You all seem to enjoy Dress-Up Day. What's the effect?"

"If it's good for our clients to loosen up by dressing down," one team member responds, "it's also good for us to tighten up by dressing up." "Dressing up every week makes me think about how I look and present myself," says another. "I like the discipline of a suit of clothes. Just as long as it's a costume I only have to wear weekly." "Wearing clothes like my clients helps me understand their world better."

"Great! So let's keep going with this thinking. When you were kids, did your family ever do a day of spring cleaning?" Some people seem to have no idea what I'm talking about, but two do remember. "Sure, our house was torn upside down, everything was cleaned, washed, and polished."

"What did it feel like?" I ask. One woman, Lisa, thinks and answers, "I had to stay home for most of a weekend and help. Our whole family was locked in until my mother declared us free. In the end it felt really good—like starting over. It was kind of a family ritual."

I thank her and say, "That's my idea—that you hold a Spring Cleaning Day." The purpose of the day, I explain, is to get the clutter to a tolerable level, produce changes in attitude about organization, and establish a ritual. "It'll be like Lisa's experience, only her mom won't be around to oversee your work. You'll have to police yourselves."

For further details I consult a few notes I've put together. "For one day you'll work alone in your offices to straighten up in any way you want. You might throw away dead files, clean up your email, go through your filing cabinets, enter information into the computer to get rid of paper, create a filing system, rearrange your space, and make repairs. Tackle anything that will make you feel as though someone opened the windows and let in crisp, clean, bright air.

"There's no need to talk to or interact with another human being all day. Your clients will be notified that the offices will be closed for inventory, but the receptionist and a skeleton crew of customer service advocates will be available for client emergencies."

"What about public spaces like conference rooms, hallways, and the cafeteria?" someone asks.

"I don't know. I'm thinking you should focus on your own space for the first day. If it's a success, then you can talk about how to tackle the rest of the space. I wouldn't be overly ambitious for the first shot. What do you think?"

There's not much discussion. Everybody decides it's a worthwhile idea and a couple of folks offer to convince the powers-that-be to sign off on the day.

The CEO's only challenge is to make the day cost effective. "If we're shutting down for a day, it better produce results," he says when a delegation brings the idea to him. "I agree this place is too cluttered, but how will we know if better organization will make any difference?"

A very junior person pipes up. "Last week I was working on the Old Boys Beer account and it took us a long time to track down the presentation we made before, to Jake's Beer. We needed that information to make sure we created something totally new for Old Boys. We finally found the files in a vacated office. It took us a whole day."

The point seems clear and the CEO sounds mildly supportive. "OK. We'll see if it works. How about a Friday before a holiday so there'll be less interruption for clients?" They agree on a date.

THE APPLICATION

I request that people take photos of their offices before, during, and after Spring Cleaning Day and post the photos on a board in the lobby. That appeals to the CEO, but my main reason for this exercise is so that the employees can see the improvement.

Jana, the woman with the 18 photos of the same dog, asks if she can talk to me. It turns out that she's reluctant to throw any of the pictures away because they are pictures of her pet; she's very attached to the dog, and having these images to look at throughout the day gives her solace.

I indicate that the clutter isn't caused by the number of pictures but by the fact that they are located on all available surfaces. We talk about alternatives. Jana's face brightens when she comes up with the idea of making a large collage to hang on the wall in front of her desk. As she measures the space I suggest that she also designate a space on one shelf to display the newest photo of her beloved dog. Every so often she can update the main photo and rearrange those in the collage. She likes the idea. "I'll arrange the collage, then take it to a framer. What a great idea."

I purposely stay away on the big day. I don't want anyone feeling as though I'm hovering about watching their efforts. On the following Monday I visit and look at the special photo board devoted to documenting the changes that have been made—impressive. Many people invite me into their spaces as well.

THE RESULTS

The wall above Jana's desk is adorned with a well-composed collage. I wonder how she got it made so fast. "Oh, I went to a frame-it-yourself place." For the time being she's also put post-it notes on many of the surfaces in her office as a self-warning: "This space is for work," "No pictures of Maggie here," and "Watch out for photo creep."

David and I talked about his office before Spring Cleaning Day and I had suggested he color-coordinate his piles. He has decided on red for hot, urgent, current work; yellow for upcoming, just-beginning projects and files from other folks; blue for recently completed projects that still require some time; and green for background info, literature searches, reference materials, and long-term projects.

"Marian, I went through every folder on the floor and put them into one of the four colored piles. I did you one better, too. I bought colored labels and wrote the title of the folder on it. I clipped the label to the folder so I can easily change it if red turns to yellow or blue or visa versa. Of course, I didn't have to go out for lunch because I had my Power Bars to eat." His own self-denigrating comment makes David roar with laughter.

Ling shows me three photos of her office in progress. The first is of a large bookcase being delivered. The second is of her on a lovely antique library ladder shelving books. The third shows Ling opening the credenza with one hand and holding folders with the other. She giggles at the third photo: "I couldn't open it before because the files were in the way." Then she shows me a fourth. The credenza is open and there are the files neatly stacked on the inside shelves. "I put all of my books in alphabetical order too."

The comments I hear throughout the morning and afternoon are gratifying and telling: "I have such a sense of accomplishment and completion." "It's like giving birth and being able to see my toes again." "I'm amazed at how much I was able to get done in just one day." "Now I can't stand to look at the clutter in public areas. I want to spring clean the rest of the space." "Just don't tell my wife I did this."

At the end of the day, when the team comes together, I challenge them: "OK, you've done a superb job here. How will you keep up the improvements you've made?"

"I wonder if we can agree to call one another on falling back into bad habits?" one person suggests. "I like that idea, but I don't want someone criticizing me if I'm having a bad day," another counters. A third person picks up with, "How about if we notice an entire week of clutter accumulation? I think that's fair. We're pretty honest here. If I notice David's red pile is mixed in with his yellow, I can say that to him. Right, David?"

I listen as they contract with one another about what is and is not all right. They agree that they want to prevent the place from returning to pre–spring cleaning chaos.

Together with the CEO, who's attending this wrap-up meeting, the team members decide to hold another Spring Cleaning Day in six months. Someone suggests once a month, but that doesn't go over very well. A few people volunteer to come in the next Saturday to clean up the public spaces. Lisa, sounding a bit like her mom, pronounces, "If we're really going to be better organized, then everywhere in the firm has to show it, not just our offices and the places where we meet with clients. So, if you want to be a part of tossing around and tightening, you'd better be here on Saturday at nine. And yes, that's a.m."

All told, they've put in several days' worth of effort and a lot of eyes roll, but almost everyone, including the CEO, shows up on the following Saturday and works diligently.

The immediate payoff was somewhat unexpected. Everyone was so proud of the improved appearance of the agency that meeting rooms became a scarce commodity. Instead of going out to clients, the members of the team began bringing clients in, and they discovered that the clients liked being at the agency because of its energy—its air of balance between creativity and control. Less time running around town meant increased time on task, which led to higher productivity and increased breakthrough thinking

Postscript: Spring Cleaning Day is a now twice-yearly ritual at this firm and continues to be the day in the office that *nobody* misses.

Language

4

Pull and Seek

SKILLS: Inquiry and advocacy

TOOL: Advocacy role play

CLUES CATEGORIES: Language, Characteristics

People are usually hired for their expertise, therefore they often operate as though the more answers they have, the more value they impart. When employees move up the ranks in management, however, the equation shifts. Not only is it important to be technically competent, people must be *strategically* competent—that is, they must be able to see the big picture, connect seemingly disparate pieces of information, and enhance the abilities of those around them.

In this story we meet an executive who is struggling to broaden her range of communication skills. She must learn to temper her predilection to advocate her position with a willingness to explore the ideas that others have to offer.

THE SITUATION

Elsa is a sales executive who has identified the area of her own behavior that she wants to work on as "being pushy." She's picked the right issue, I think to myself, although I might not use those exact words to describe her behavior.

I ask Elsa how she has determined that being pushy is a problem for her.

"Well, the marketing people argue with me a lot. They make remarks, too. Like, 'Elsa, why don't you just *tell* us what we'll do.' Then I noticed that a couple of people in our department don't show me their proposals any more. I hear it's because I'm too critical in the way I give feedback. I only want to make things better, but how I'm going about it seems to have the opposite effect."

We talk for some time and (with her permission, of course) I observe Elsa in action to gather further evidence. She certainly appears to be very good at reading signs of dissatisfaction and frustration in those she works with, but I want to confirm her own analysis of the problem before moving ahead.

I attend meetings with Elsa to see how she behaves and, sure enough, she's right. She's usually the first to speak up. She doesn't interrupt people, but she speaks as though what she says is fact and need not be questioned. This attitude has a tendency to shut down discussion. Also, Elsa rarely asks questions. Although she can listen with great intensity if others are willing to venture a thought or an opinion, she then leaps ahead immediately to suggest an action in response.

On the other hand, Elsa is one of the top sales performers in the company and she seems to enjoy very warm personal relationships with people. In the course of one of the meetings I attended, one colleague thanked her profusely for getting his wife an appointment with a high-profile physician, and another gave her a hug to congratulate her on signing a very big contract.

THE APPROACH

I have hunches about Elsa, but that isn't a good road to pursue for a coach, so I decide to begin with a few standard assessment instruments to profile her style. When we talk about her profile Elsa is fascinated and very interested in what she can do to minimize some of her extremes. I tell her we'll work toward gaining access to "unpracticed behaviors"—social skills she may need to acquire or may already possess but rarely uses in the workplace. I like to see my clients expand rather than shrink their repertoire of social skills. Instead of exhorting people to labor over breaking existing habits that are getting in their way, I've had greater success in encouraging them to replace these routine behaviors with new ones. It seems that in the process of incorporating fresh ways of acting into daily life we gradually and naturally let go of stale, unhelpful behavioral patterns with relatively little inner struggle or conflict.

(When I first encountered this philosophy in business, I recognized it instantly from my own experience with a coach in a different context. As a young tennis player I had developed several bad habits from learning the game only through playing it—no lessons, but lots of mimicking seasoned players. Finally I somehow became good enough to play in club tournaments. But when I won, I really didn't know why, and the same thing went for when I lost. Then a new indoor club opened in our town and I decided to take lessons with its pro. He watched me play and never said much about my game. He did show me a different way of swinging, however, which I practiced under his tutelage. It didn't take me long to swing like that all of the time. I couldn't have gone back to the old grab bag of techniques if I'd tried. My game, consistency, and enjoyment improved. That type of result is what I aim for when I coach.)

I ask Elsa to describe the person she sees from the assessment instruments.

"Strong personality, bias for action, quick movement into problem solving, goes through people to get things done, and likes to be in charge. Like I said, I'm pushy."

I follow up with an inquiry about how she'd like to be.

"I certainly don't want to go to the opposite extreme—I don't want to be laid back. I still want to be the person who sells the most, but I don't want to chew up my colleagues in the process. I guess if I had to name it, I'd say I want to be more collaborative. I hate the term 'team player,' by the way."

"Why?"

"Not all sports are meant to be played by a team. And it's such a trendy term."

I share some additional insights into her profile, probe more about the team player remark, and feel ready to move on.

Elsa is complex. I don't want to reduce her confidence or urge her to try to be someone she is not. She reminds me of a man I once coached who knew the answers to almost any question he was asked and couldn't accept the fact that his job in life was not providing answers for the whole world, no matter what the topic. It took us months to move him out of the "answer man" role into being a sought-after resource who could provide knowledge when it was needed and wanted.

I can see now that Elsa's habit of wanting to make things better is actually blocking that from happening for her. She is so eager to sell ideas to people—prospects, customers, direct reports, and colleagues—that it's touching. She's just as eager to improve herself, so we agree to move as quickly as we can.

Initially we contract for me to be with her for two days, to mirror back what I observe, offer new skills to practice, and monitor progress. Over the next three weeks we'll talk every other day, then I'll return to her site for a day to observe her on the job again. That's very concentrated work. Once she gets the heavy initial dose, we can gradually practice and strengthen.

In my experience I've witnessed two kinds of leaders: push and pull. "Push" leaders set a direction and propel people toward it. The "Do it my way or the highway" autocrat is an extreme example of a push leader. They can be very effective at getting work accomplished, but the emotional environment they create is usually stressful and results can be short-lived.

Elsa has a tendency to be a push leader. She sees a goal and lunges toward it with head down and nostrils flaring. To her credit, more often than not the effort is on target. The problem is that others don't know how she arrived at the goal, what their role is in reaching it, or how it fits into a bigger picture. Her movements are so quick and definitive that there's no room for analysis, options, questions, or involvement.

A couple of hefty failures might humble Elsa enough to stop her in her tracks, but letting that happen would be neither a positive nor a productive way to foster growth.

Elsa's description of how she'd like to be is that of a "pull" leader: She wants to enlist people in moving in parallel toward a goal. I ask her to use a sports analogy to describe the leader she envisions. She wouldn't like to be the captain of a hockey team—too chaotic, huge interdependencies, contentious. The Davis Cup is more fitting, she says—individual contributors playing their best, coached by the captain, plus high-profile winning.

I also suspect that Elsa is tired of being alone. It hurts her that people shy away from working with her. She is a people person who also sees the world as a set of problems to solve.

So, like the tennis pro, I analyze her game and decide to focus on the skills of inquiry and acknowledgment to improve her swing.

To start with, I give her the Pennies Transfer tool to practice acknowledgment: Beginning each morning with ten pennies in a left-hand pocket, every time she acknowledges someone's contribution, knowledge, experience, positive attitude, feelings, or hard work, she transfers a penny to a right-hand pocket; the goal is to get that transfer going. (*See* Chapter 12.)

After a day or two of using this tool with ease and immediate success (remember, she's very tuned into people and is achievement oriented), Elsa says that she's psyched to move on.

Moving her to the other skill, inquiry, is more difficult. Inquiry—the solicitation and examination of ideas to increase understanding—is a highly evolved skill for anyone. Few people naturally pause during interactions to look at an issue through various lenses. Elsa, in particular, has such a bias for decisiveness and action that I suspect she won't even know what inquiry is at first, let alone how to use it.

I begin by asking Elsa to describe how she approaches her work: "When you're given a problem to solve, what steps do you take to resolve it?" After some probing from me, Elsa uncovers the fact that she feels powerful when she can come up with an answer and weak when she doesn't know what direction to take. "I get to the bottom of problems very fast and

I think it's my responsibility to share what I would do to solve them. Problems are real."

"What are the strengths and weaknesses of that approach?"

"All right, let's see. The strengths are that people hear what I think, gain options based on my experience, have a path to follow, can add to my suggestions, and know where I stand. And they come to me when something practical must be decided."

"And the weaknesses?"

"People don't always come up with their own ideas and they depend on me to have all the answers. But I could have the wrong solution, and it reduces their willingness to chime in and to take risks. And so, well, not all ideas are considered. There are probably loads more that I ignore. Oh, and people will go elsewhere for strategic decisions. I can become pigeon-holed."

"As what?"

"As a fixer, not a big-picture thinker. I don't want that. I want to be both. How do I do that?"

"Remember, we're trying to replace old, counter-productive habits with new ones. So, let's turn your attention to keeping the good and adding to it. We want to widen the spectrum of available responses. I've got another tool to suggest."

"Excellent. I like the idea of addition rather than subtraction. Will this tool be like Pennies Transfer?"

"Not really. That's a very clear tool to apply because there's a physical element to it and you immediately see the results of your actions. What I'm about to propose is a mind shift as well as a skill. It's not really a tool; it's more of a remodeling kit."

"I just hope it doesn't require brain surgery."

"Sorry, I don't mean to make it sound so dire. What you usually do is *give* suggestions. That's advocacy—taking a position and communicating it. All leaders must be able to advocate."

"I totally agree. There are too many people in this company who won't take a stance. Someone has to take the initiative of advocating a solution to a problem."

"The trick is," I tell Elsa, "balancing advocacy with other behaviors that enlist people more. Pull leaders instinctively,

and also through learning, know how to engage people—they pull others into their wake. They need to learn to use inquiry too, which balances out reliance on advocacy. In other words, they need to try to find out what's going on to create as large a picture as possible before deciding on a course of action."

She resists a bit. "Inquiry sounds so legal—you know, an inquiry into the so-and-so scandal."

"Well, that's not so far-fetched. To inquire means to explore meaning. It's a deceptively simple notion," I explain, "yet it's not practiced nearly as widely as advocacy. I think that's because people believe their job is to have answers and be experts. In reality, people who explore thinking and options are much more apt to gain buy-in, to help others grow, and to come up with big ideas. It takes a lot of self-confidence to examine and reflect before acting."

Elsa comes back with, "Reflection takes time—time we don't have. I can't imagine a meeting where we'd sit around asking each other questions. Everyone would get fed up and we'd accomplish nothing."

Now we're getting somewhere, I think.

THE APPLICATION

"Would you like to test that assumption?" I ask.

"Sure. Do you mean now? How can we do that?"

"Let's try. Play along with me. A peer comes to you with a freshly minted proposal and asks for your feedback. What would you do?"

"I'd ask who the client is, what my peer is trying to accomplish, and what's the timeframe. Then I'd read it and tell him what I think based on that info."

"What's the purpose of your first few questions?"

"I want to understand the context of the proposal." There's a new tone in Elsa's voice.

"Terrific. What's your role in reading the proposal?"

"Let's see. My peer is asking for advice, the proposal could be better, I have expertise that my peer doesn't have. My role is to cut to the chase and help improve the proposal."

"Fine. Now, what other assumptions about your role could you have? After all, an assumption is just an untested belief."

"This is harder," says Elsa. "What assumptions? I have expertise that would be useful to my peer. My ideas are valuable. And, oh yeah, the biggest one of all, my peer actually wants my analysis of the situation and advice about how to approach it. I guess there's another assumption—my peer isn't capable of solving the problem himself."

"And now, how about different assumptions? Ones that put the other person in a better, more able light?" I ask.

"All right. This person doesn't want advice, the proposal is fine as it is, we both have expertise, and the best use of my time is to, is to—I don't know what."

Elsa stops in frustration. "This is hard. I guess I could assume it's time efficient to talk about the proposal in hopes it will save bother later on. But there usually isn't time to get back to it later. I guess that's another assumption. Hmmm." She falls silent.

"Good. For the sake of thinking differently about the situation, Elsa, suppose you decided to act on your second set of assumptions about your peer, those that infer that your role is to be a partner instead of an improver. What actions would you take then?"

"I could ask if he's satisfied with the proposal or what areas of the proposal he's not sure about. I guess I could also ask what he thinks I might know that's not included in the proposal."

"You're right. You're beginning to get the hang of this. Do you want to role-play the situation? I'll be your peer and you begin by asking questions."

We role-play and Elsa does real well for the first two questions: "Are there any areas of the proposal you're not sure about?" and "How can I add to the proposal?" Then she sees an opportunity to offer expert advice, but she cleverly couches it as a question: "Don't you think it would be a good idea to talk about our track record in their industry?"

I point out to her that, although the statement ends with a question mark, it's still advocacy. She's leading her "partner." Elsa is such a conscientious person that she just laughs at herself.

The next day I notice that Elsa is trying like crazy to ask more questions. Still she holds the mindset that her job is to have answers, so her questions are pointed rather than exploratory. She's not very interested in helping others find their own answers. She's using questions to maneuver people into her web. This is going to be a tough transition.

But we'll keep practicing her new swing until it becomes natural. I propose we conduct another role-play. This time, Elsa and a peer from marketing are going to make a joint presentation to a potential customer.

"OK, Elsa. You start." I sit back with my hands in my lap.

Elsa begins, "Frank, what do you think our presentation should be like?"

Replying as Frank, I say, "I'm not sure I know what you're asking. Do you mean the content, format, style? Help me out here."

"All three. Let's start with the purpose of the presentation. What you do see as our purpose in pitching this guy?"

"We're trying to get his business. That's the purpose," I respond with a tinge of impatience in my voice.

Elsa goes on, "Right. OK, now let's move on to the content. What are the top two selling points? What's in it for the customer?"

I stop the role-play and ask Elsa to go back to her response to Frank's statement, "We're trying to get his business. That's the purpose."

"Is that the only purpose?" I ask.

"Probably not."

"Then how come you didn't inquire further?" I want to know.

"It seemed like a good enough answer. Frank didn't seem like he has much tolerance for your inquiry stuff. He and I were both anxious to move on with the content. What's the point of listing all of the other purposes there might be?"

"Good inquiry. What do *you* think?"

"You answered a question with a question. I find that annoying. It's like you're skirting the issue."

"What might I have said instead?"

"There you go again. You could have given me the value of

listing the purposes. You could have answered the question that I asked."

"You're right, Elsa. I could have given my opinion. Sometimes that's called for. But right now I'm trying to shift the work from me to you. I don't want to be the supplier of information; I want you to generate the ideas. I see my role as being the catalyst for your thinking."

Elsa pauses and says, "All right. I'll go along with that for now. In that case, let's see. Go back to the purpose question. Is the only purpose of our presentation a sale?"

I continue as her peer, Frank. Elsa is definitely improving and I can see her mental wheels turning in her effort to keep the interaction balanced between inquiry and advocacy.

We role-play for an hour every day for several days. I throw high and low balls and watch Elsa swing differently at each. Still, she struggles with these new ideas about her role. It's scary for her to give up the belief that she's paid to have answers. But as I also observe her interacting with others I can see that she's making progress.

For example, while I'm in her office one afternoon a VP from another department calls to talk about the efficacy of opening a satellite office in Asia. Elsa starts with, "Before we begin to entertain any ideas about the solution, let's be clear about what problems the proposal is addressing." When I walk out after ten minutes they're still examining his responses to her initial inquiry.

THE RESULTS

It would be fantasyland for me to say that Elsa has become a new type of problem solver after only a month. First of all, she's got her tendencies to contend with. Elsa likes to be in charge, move fast, and puzzle out dense problems on her own. Secondly, the organization is used to her the way she is. Other people count on her to move things along. There's no immediate reinforcement for Elsa to be more strategic in her thinking. Additionally, the organization is faced with a shrinking market and it needs decisive risk-takers to keep it afloat.

The shift that I observe is less initial advocacy. Instead, Elsa often begins interactions with open, probing questions. That way she and her thinking partner can discover what they're really talking about in their interaction. Once the playing field is outlined, Elsa provides ideas. This upfront loading of the interaction brings both parties to similar understandings of the problem and issues. Additionally, the scope of the question at hand can be widened if there are ancillary issues that should be addressed, or it can be narrowed if it's too broad. Once it's apparent to me that Elsa has added more inquiry to her interactions, I suggest that she actually begin to use the terms "advocacy" and "inquiry."

"Do you mean," she asks, "that I should actually say, 'I have an inquiry about…' or 'I'm advocating…'?"

"Yes, Elsa, that is exactly what I mean," I reply. "When you can differentiate your thinking, why not let others know? To be more precise, if you have a position of advocacy and state it, those listening will know your agenda and can listen knowing that you believe in an idea or direction. But if you're not ready to make a decision and need to look more deeply into an issue, saying you have an inquiry enables others to listen with that point of view. Both you and the listeners will know where to head."

In our fifth month of working together, Elsa is promoted to executive vice-president of sales *and* marketing. When she asks the CEO of her company why, he tells her it's because her thinking has matured. He explains that he has confidence she can represent both departments when it's time to analyze a situation. "You're slower on the trigger. I need people around me who can see a problem in its entirety. You're less of a pit bull now, more of a border collie."

At month eight I'm once again in Elsa's office and with her permission I eavesdrop on a telephone conversation. This is what I hear her say: "Now that we're fully conversant with the Asian market, I advocate that we form the strategic alliance with the AsiaAll Group that X has proposed. By the way, I learned a lot from you about how market dominance has shifted in Asia over the last decade. Thank you. Before we go to press with this announcement, let's spend some time exploring loose ends we may not be seeing. My first inquiry is, 'What might be brewing in Korea that we could use to sow the seeds of increased market share there?'"

Advocacy, acknowledgment, and inquiry in one brief interaction. Elsa seems to have her new swing down pat.

5

Loop the Loop

SKILL: Listening

TOOL: The listening loop

CLUES CATEGORIES: Language, Underlying motives

*I*t's always shocking for people to learn that what they think they said and what people hear are not the same. Worse, actions are taken on these assumptions. The outcome can be confusing, humorous, and sometimes disastrous.

In this story we witness communication misfiring between a CEO and his direct reports.

THE SITUATION

Philip Engleston is the new CEO of a company that I'll call Protect, a defense contractor. He's a rarity in the industry because he came from a non-defense company. Historically, people who run these companies are insiders—most often individuals who are trained as engineers, who understand the military and the government, and who are very connected in Washington.

The arrival of this new man sends ripples throughout the organization, especially at the senior level. I've been coaching

a team of executives, five men and one woman, for about a year and they regard Philip as an unknown quantity; in their highly regulated world, this makes them wary.

They'd like to continue the project they were tasked to do by the outgoing CEO: to analyze how technology is transferred within the organization and develop recommendations to make it a consistent capability. They don't know what Philip thinks about the project, or about them, for that matter.

This particular project is of high value because the company is losing time and money to redundancies and waste. In the defense industry, some information cannot migrate from one division of an organization to another because government regulations prevent the sharing of certain kinds of knowledge even within the same company. So although in general it seems like a good idea to facilitate the transfer of technological knowledge, certain information must be protected, and many employees are so cautious that they don't share any technological information at all, even when the regulations would allow them to do so. This team is charged with figuring out what can be shared and how.

Within his first month on the job, Philip Engleston sends the following memo to the team (I have been sent a copy and invited to attend):

The purpose of the meeting is for me to talk to the Technology Transfer Team about how I want to use your team. I will also talk about my business philosophy, my goals for the company, and my thoughts about technology transfer. I intend to hold similar small meetings with other key leaders throughout the organization.

I look forward to our meeting on Wednesday, February 9 at 8 a.m. in the executive conference room. It is not necessary to bring any of your project work with you.

There is lots of speculation about the memo, but mercifully there are only two days until the meeting. The CEO is punctual, he talks solidly for one hour, and at the conclusion he says, "I don't want to entertain questions right now. As you go forward, it matters to me that you pay attention to what I said today. I think the technology transfer work you're doing is very important, and I want you to continue." His departure is polite and quick.

THE APPROACH

The team sits in silence, seeming somewhat stunned. I break the ice with, "Let's create a list of the things you believe you heard Philip say."

"Marian, that's wasting our time," one team member says. "We all know what Philip said."

"What do other people think?"

The majority of people agree. "We all know what he said. Our job is to figure out how to implement his direction. And to go on with our project."

One team member directs a question to me. "What's behind your suggestion of writing down what we think Philip said? You never make a suggestion to us without a reason or hunch."

I smile at their awareness of the methods we've been using together. "You guys know me pretty well after a year. I'm not comfortable that we all do know what he said. Furthermore, before you plow forward with your project, I suggest you check to see if the direction you've set is aligned with Philip's goals. Even though he told you to move forward, I'm not confident that we know what that means. Better to spend an hour now than a hundred hours later."

"OK," says the person who spoke first. "That's probably important, but I don't want to belabor the point if we're all in sync."

Then, as they chart what they heard Philip say, they are flabbergasted at the wide range of responses.

"How come we have so many different opinions about what was actually said in just 60 minutes?"

"We're the six most senior people in the company," another team member says. "What would happen if we each acted on what we *thought* Philip said? It's alarming."

"Obviously Philip thought he was crystal clear," a third adds. "So clear, in fact, that he didn't ask for any questions after he talked to us."

This is my cue. "What questions would you have asked?"

"At the time, we had no clue about how differently we interpreted his messages, so questions didn't seem necessary."

"Well, we might at least have gotten clarity had we asked the right questions." They've repeatedly heard my diatribe about the importance of asking excellent questions.

From another team member: "Now I'm concerned about moving forward with our project. What can we do?"

I pose another question. "How open do you think Philip is to coming back to talk with you again? And if you want to ask him, how do you think he'll perceive the request?"

After a short discussion, they agree that it is critical to reengage Philip. They also believe that he'll think less of them because of it, but that's preferable to acting without clarity. They ask me if I'll be the one to invite him to come back. I refuse. "If you want him back you have to make the case. If I were to do it, he might wonder why you didn't step up to ask him yourselves. Let's think about how you can do that."

To my delight, they take time to craft an invitation to Philip. In our work together I've tried to emphasize learning to aim before they shoot. When we first met, they were so action biased that the moment somebody suggested something they all latched on to it and out the door they went with abandon.

The following day the designated point person tells me, "Philip called me right after he got our memo. He wanted to know what was behind it. I told him about the exercise we did—capturing his ideas after his talk—and how far apart we all were. I said we all felt we'd be making a huge mistake in taking action based on six varying points of view. We need to be clear about the charge that we're being given. 'You're executives,' he said. 'You're the next in line. If you don't understand what I'm asking you to do, who will? I'd like to see that list you're talking about—the one that spells out what you *think* I said.'"

Surprisingly, I also receive a call from Philip himself. "I'm disturbed. These are senior executives. I've given them a very simple charge and they don't seem to understand what it is. What's the problem here?"

I take a deep breath. "How long did you work with the same executive team in your previous company?" I ask.

"Most of the people were with me for about five years."

"Can you recall what it was like to work with them initially?"

"OK, I get your point. But you must know, Marian, this company is really asleep at the wheel. We don't have time to make nice-nice. I've got a short rope here. Not much time to awaken them."

"Just what in your interaction with this team makes you think they're asking for 'nice-nice'?" I ask, with a hint of challenge in my voice. "And what *is* that anyway?"

"Polite talk. Not saying what's on your mind. Everyone here is so deliberate and cautious. I don't want my six senior executives to pussyfoot around. I expect them to be able to run with the ball."

"Philip, I hear a lot of dangerous assumptions in that statement."

"Like what? Is this what you do when you coach the team?"

I decide that since Phil respects directness, I might as well ask, "Do you mind if I ask how you regard me?" After all, he's inherited my contract to work with the company.

"Look, Marian, I have no beef with you. I understand you're doing an excellent job with this team. I'm neither patient nor politic. I have a big job to do in a short amount of time. I don't want to handhold the six most senior guys in the company. By the way, what assumptions are you talking about?"

"Since you ask, here are the assumptions I heard: being deliberate and cautious is bad; the only way to move this company is through fast action; and desiring clarity is a sign of weakness. And what do you think the team is asking for that's unreasonable?"

"You got that from what I said? Hmmm." He pauses. "I think the team is asking to have direction set out so clearly that they won't make any mistakes. That isn't possible. Executives should be able to act without everything spelled out for them."

"Philip, there's a huge difference between wanting to align with your direction and having everything spelled out. You've just met these people. What's causing such concern about their asking a few questions?"

"OK, OK. I need these guys. And I definitely need them to be my eyes and ears right now. If they want more time with me to set direction, they'll have it." Then he throws the challenge right back at me. "What's your role in all of this?"

"If you were an author," I say, drawing on one of my favorite metaphors (after all, he's given me an opening), "you certainly wouldn't want somebody to translate your work into another language and deviate from the plot, characters, or message. This team is going to be your translator. My goal is to make sure that the translation is accurate and well executed. The more precise we can make the language, the less room for misinterpretation there is. This is a difficult transition time for everyone. How it's handled will shape your tenure at the company."

Philip says nothing for a moment. Then, "Thank you for your candor. I'll set up another meeting within the next few days."

THE APPLICATION

To Philip's credit, the meeting is scheduled within three days and when he comes into the room he asks how the team wants to use the time.

"Marian developed a protocol that seems quite efficient," says one team member. "Let her explain it to you to see if it makes sense to you as well."

Philip nods and I begin.

"I propose that we go over the now famous list point by point. It's summarized here on the board. You can read a statement, and say 'That's what I mean' or 'You have a different interpretation of what I mean, let me clarify' or 'I mean something diametrically opposed, let me give you my point once more.' We'll use three different colors to highlight what arises. Green indicates we're in sync; orange calls for clarification; and red sounds the alarm—we're on different planets. If you're in sync, no further words are necessary. The rest will require give-and-take discussion until clarity is reached. What do you think?"

It's clear that Philip thinks this is all a bit much; maybe the

color coding strikes him as being hokey. But he's game. "Let's start," he says.

For the next hour Philip and the six people work on the list. At the beginning about 40 percent of the items on the board are green (already in sync), only 10 percent are red (we've got a problem), and the rest are bright orange (need clarification). Clarity increases as the group moves along and sees how Philip's thoughts are interconnected. It's obvious to me that the more the team probes, the clearer and more articulate Philip becomes.

After an hour, I think the meeting has gone on long enough and to bring it to closure I suggest, "Before you leave, write three highlights of Philip's message. This is a test of clarity."

Within five minutes the team members post their highlights. This time 80 percent are green, there are no reds, and the rest are orange. Philip seems ready to talk about the orange again, but before he can begin I hold up my hand and ask the group what isn't clear. During the brief interchange that follows, we discover that people actually understand these points, they just aren't all that pleased with them. However, we've done enough for the day. I capture their questions and concerns for Philip to think about over the next few days. He promises to get back to the team and leaves.

The next day Philip asks me to stop by his office. There's a smile on his face. "I want to institute that process we did yesterday. Please write it up so that we can use it widely. It's very efficient and increases understanding dramatically. We talked about some tough issues and it wasn't personal. I was amazed at how we moved so quickly to a green list."

THE RESULTS

Philip and the senior team continue to use a version of the Listening Loop most times when they meet to talk about an issue or strategy. I've noticed that their initial discussions are like a rough draft, then they use the Listening Loop to focus their thinking and sharpen their language.

Within this organization, the underlying motive of increasing the likelihood of sound decisions is realized every time the

Listening Loop is used. And a higher demand for clarity inevitably translates into more rigorous thinking. At least, this is how it works within the top management echelon.

Despite Philip's directive, at lower levels within the company groups aren't allowing (or being allowed) sufficient time to go through the full process. I don't have a mandate to intervene, so I watch warily. I keep urging the seniors to model using the tool. If they always use it with others it will eventually become the norm.

The sales force has invented one of the most successful adaptations of the Listening Loop. They give potential customers sticky notes at the beginning of a sales pitch and ask them to jot down questions and concerns. At the end of the presentation, the salesperson and the potential customer make a list of what was said that hit the mark, what missed, and what wasn't clear. This technique both gives the salesperson an outline of how to respond to the customer's concerns and engages the customer in the selling process.

One member of another team tells me that she has begun using the tool with her teenage kids at home. It's amazing, she says, what they tuned out at first and how much more attentive they've become.

The Listening Loop starts out as a tool and ends up as a way of being. Eventually people who use this tool become so accustomed to "checking back for meaning" that they do so as an ingrained practice—a valuable habit in an increasingly diverse world.

Underlying Motives

6

Met to Death

SKILL: Meeting management

TOOL: Time use matrix

CLUES CATEGORIES: Underlying motives, Energy

Teamwork and communication are vital in any organization, but in some cases the amount of time people spend in meetings is not only daunting, it may interfere with their ability to plan and execute the work they've been hired to do. And while many people may conclude, after serving on this team or that committee, that not all meetings add value, all too often they still feel obliged to attend.

The manager in this story is so swamped with meetings that she has to do the rest of her job outside of working hours. To help her gain some control over her life, I offer her a tool for evaluating whether a particular meeting is a good use of her time.

THE SITUATION

Pamela could be the poster child for "good corporate citizen." She chairs her organization's Universal Charity Fund Drive, founded its Summer Family Sports Program, sits on the Sustainability Board, and manages the New Marketing Initiatives Team.

She's also the director of marketing in a large not-for-profit enterprise. A director-level position puts its occupant above manager and below the vice-presidential level of an organization. In my experience, these jobs are extremely difficult because the individuals who hold them are squeezed between two layers of management with different, and sometimes competing, agendas. Vice-presidents want their directors to translate their strategies to a larger audience and to ensure that they are carried out. In many cases, however, lower-level managers want these same directors to let the divisional VPs know just how unrealistic their strategies and demands are. Even when things are going reasonably well, people at the director level are always scrambling to find the resources to get work done as quickly and efficiently as possible while pleasing two constituencies, the people above and below them in the hierarchy of the organization.

When Pamela calls to ask for my help, she says that she's overextended and no longer seems able to put the elements of her work life into priority order. At our initial meeting she tells me an all-too-familiar story.

"I leave for work at 6.30 in the morning," she says, "and rarely get home before 8. Sometimes I'm sending emails at 2 a.m. *And* I work on Saturdays."

"Why do you work those hours?"

"It's the only way I can make a dent in the amount of work I have. Even so, I'm always behind."

"May I look at your calendar?" I ask.

"Sure." She hands me a PDA.

I see days filled with meeting after meeting, with little else entered.

"Wow, you sure attend a lot of meetings. Tell me about that."

"My work involves coordinating different sets of people who represent different parts of the organization, and to accomplish any of the tasks I'm handed I usually have to work across several functions. For example, if we're going to market a new service, I've got to make sure the financials are sound,

and I have to position it so we're not cannibalizing any other service; then I have to help the tech writers grasp the offering and make sure that the call center personnel understand the service well enough to explain it to our members.

"I've tried bringing everyone who's affected together for one meeting, but it was always a logistical nightmare and people complained about much of the information being irrelevant to their own particular jobs. So now I meet with each of the groups involved separately so we can focus on their piece of the pie."

"What about all these other committees you're on?"

"It's like getting into the college of your choice. If you want to be promoted, you've got to be involved in extracurricular activities. There are more directors than VPs. The higher up you go the more the field narrows; the people who get the top jobs are those with the most visibility and that means task forces and projects."

I ask the key question, "Do you really want anything to be different or am I here merely to listen to your woes?"

Her response is sincere. "Yes, I want things to be different, and I want to be a vice-president. But I don't know how I can do both."

THE APPROACH

"First of all," I begin, "let's assess the value and importance of the meetings you attend. It might well be that you can reduce the number of meetings and buy some time. At the very least, we should be able to examine your work schedule and establish some priorities. Are you game?"

Pamela's extremely enthusiastic. "You bet. I'm miserable, my kids are furious, my work is out of control, and my husband is losing patience."

"OK. Let's begin with listing your job objectives. What *must* you accomplish—what are your job needs? For now let's exclude what you'd *like* to get done—your wants. Just differentiating between your needs and wants can be illuminating. What would you say is the difference?"

"Gee, Marian, I don't know if I can separate them. How about if we list all of my objectives then we can sort them into needs and wants."

I give Pamela credit for that modification. She begins her list.

"Increase market share, build awareness about the organization in currently underserved markets, become a VP, build capability in my direct reports, work with technology folks to develop marketing systems, serve the community, influence colleagues in other departments, get more work done in less time, involve the New Market Initiatives Team in departmental strategy, hand off Summer Family Sports, spend more time with my family, increase my visibility throughout the organization. How's that for starters?"

I smile and say, "You sure have a large appetite. Now let's see if we can break that list down into a few categories."

"Do you mean like work and personal? I think there are several within work and maybe only one in personal."

We talk back and forth to define categories and I make some comments to help Pamela clarify her thinking. For example, I don't think that there's any real difference between "increase market share" and "build awareness about the organization in currently underserved markets." Pamela concludes that building market share has several aspects to it, only one of which is to build awareness about the organization in currently underserved markets.

As Pamela hears herself think she realizes that she doesn't group or coordinate her work. She approaches each task as though it were unique and discrete instead of connected to other projects, past and present. The result is redundancy and waste. It's wasteful for Pamela to approach every new project from scratch. She's not transferring her experience and knowledge from one task to another.

Once we've identified this tendency to jump from project to project without looking for similarities, I ask what the reason might be. Pamela says she has so much to do that there's no time for reflection.

Furthermore, she adds, "I'm known for my ability to get things done, and that gets you much further in this organization than being known for integrating ideas. If someone were to walk past my desk and see me just sitting and thinking, I'd be asked what I was doing, not what was I thinking about." She pauses. "But I do agree that I could work more efficiently."

I recall learning about action-oriented and reflection-oriented people in a graduate school course. Pamela certainly fits the action-oriented profile: She's someone who wants to get things accomplished, achieve results, and keep on the move. This bias, plus working for an understaffed not-for-profit, adds up to one frenetically busy lady.

We return to the categorization process and end up with the following job objectives:

- ❏ Increase market share.
- ❏ Develop direct reports.
- ❏ Build organization-wide cross-functional systems.
- ❏ Position self for VP slot.
- ❏ Establish information networks.

We do not include community involvement or work–life balance as objectives. Community involvement is an avenue through which to achieve some of the objectives Pamela has listed. Work–life balance is a result of how she does her job: If she improves her efficiency, she'll have more time available for her personal life.

Next we return to her calendar to identify the activities that Pamela engages in over a week. I notice that her days aren't actually filled to the capacity that she describes. She does have a lot of meetings, but it seems that she's not spending her unscheduled time productively. To prepare for our next weekly coaching session, I assign Pamela the task of recording everything she does in a day so that we can really see how every minute is spent.

What an eye-opener that is for Pamela. "I cannot *believe* how my days evaporate," she says as we begin our next session. "When I write down everything I do, there are more unscheduled time-eaters than anything else. People have absolutely no respect for my time."

I respond, "Maybe *you* don't have any respect for your time. Who's in control anyway?"

Pamela wrinkles up her face and asks me to explain what I mean.

"Pamela," I say, "in my experience I have never seen an organization or a person's co-workers say 'We're asking too much' or 'I'm usurping Pamela's time.' They are as greedy for what you can offer as you allow them to be. Does that make sense to you?"

"Yes, yes it does," she replies. Then she brightens. "So many light bulbs have just gone off. I think about James, a peer who recently became a father. When he returned from paternity leave, he announced that for the next six months he'd be leaving work at 5 p.m. because of the change in his home situation. Sure, people gossiped about it, but in the end his department adjusted to his schedule. As far as I know, people still think he's doing a good job."

Pamela stops to think. "But if your hypothesis is correct, that I'm always accommodating the expectations and demands of others, how do I change that? I bet you're going to say that I have to change *me*. I think your point is that I'm the one who's allowed the situation to get out of control, so I'm the only one who can get it back in line. Right?"

THE APPLICATION

I congratulate her for being astute and suggest that we continue with our analysis of her time. "Even though you're beginning to see what you've created and some things you might change, there's nothing like getting it all down in black and white. Once you have the complete picture laid out before you, you can do a proper analysis of how you spend your time and then you can begin to make modifications. OK to move on?"

We return to the PDA and begin to list the activities in which Pamela is currently involved:

Job tasks
Develop marketing strategies, various projects
Create and monitor budgets
Collaborate with other departments
Work with IT to develop marketing systems
Provide ongoing feedback to direct reports

Formal meetings
New Marketing Initiatives Team
Cross-functional projects
Universal Charity Fund
Summer Family Sports Program
Weekly departmental status meeting
Bi-weekly meeting with boss
Rotating performance reviews

Informal meetings
Office drop-ins
Telephone consults
Hallway encounters
Lunch dates

Professional development
On-site graduate marketing class
PowerPoint computer training workshop
Work with mentor
Four-days-per-month leadership development program
Work with coach

By the time Pamela finishes this daunting list of activities she's in tears. She can't believe the complexity of her work life. "No wonder I always feel as though I can't accomplish half of what is on my morning to-do list. I've created an impossible situation for myself. I absolutely have to let go of some stuff here. What do you recommend?"

I demur. "It's not my job we're talking about, it's yours. Only *you* can decide what stays and goes. I can help you discover the problems and options, but I would never presume to make choices for you. You must take ownership of your own time."

Nevertheless, helping her do just that is why I'm here, so I continue. "I can and do suggest one more piece of self-examination. You've spelled out your objectives and listed your activities. Now I think you need to develop criteria for deciding if an activity is of value, a method for weighing the importance of an activity. For example, you know that it's extremely important to develop marketing strategies—it's part of your basic job description. But why else is that activity important? What other criteria might it satisfy? Is that clear?"

"Let me say what I think you mean," Pamela offers. "I need to look at each of the things I do now and decide if it meets a job objective. I get that part, but I'm not sure I understand about the other criteria. What others are there?"

"That would be the first criterion, whether this activity meets a job objective. The others are up to you. Think about it. What others come to mind?"

Pamela is hesitant at first. "Do I like doing the activity? Do I learn from it?" Then she picks up speed. "Is there an immediate application? Is there a long-term payoff? Does it add to the overall progress of the organization? Who benefits from my being involved? Should I be the one to handle it or can someone else do it?"

I suggest that we begin to build a time-use matrix. Pamela's job objectives are given letter designations and written down the left-hand side of a large sheet of paper; the activities are listed across the top. The criteria are numbered and written on the bottom, like the legend for a map. She chooses six criteria, and, at my suggestion, includes "not applicable" as a seventh:

1 Meets objective
2 Personal enjoyment
3 Learning opportunity
4 Immediate application
5 Long-term payoff
6 Cannot be delegated
7 Not applicable

| | Formal meetings | | | | | | |
| | Activities | | | | | | |
Objectives	NMI Team	Cross-functional projects	Universal Charity Fund	Summer Family Sports Program	Weekly departmental status meeting	Bi-weekly meeting with boss	Rotating performance reviews
A Increase market share	1, 2, 3, 4, 5, 6						
B Develop direct reports	7						
C Build cross-functional systems	1, 3, 5						
D Position self for VP slot	1, 2, 5, 6						
E Establish information networks	1, 3, 4, 5						

Criteria: 1 Meets objective; 2 Personal enjoyment; 3 Learning opportunity; 4 Immediate application; 5 Long-term payoff; 6 Cannot be delegated; 7 Not applicable

Now she's ready to rate each activity: At the intersection of an objective and an activity she will enter the numbers of any of the criteria that apply to that intersection.

As a trial she makes her first entries under "Formal meetings: New Marketing Initiatives (NMI) team":

Formal meetings							
Objectives	**Activities**						
	NMI Team	Cross-functional projects	Universal Charity Fund	Summer Family Sports Program	Weekly depart-mental status meeting	Bi-weekly meeting with boss	Rotating perform-ance reviews
A Increase market share	1, 2, 3, 4, 5, 6						
B Develop direct reports	7						
C Build cross-functional systems	1, 3, 5						
D Position self for VP slot	1, 2, 5, 6						
E Establish information networks	1, 3, 4, 5						

Criteria: 1 Meets objective; 2 Personal enjoyment; 3 Learning opportunity; 4 Immediate application; 5 Long-term payoff; 6 Cannot be delegated; 7 Not applicable

When she finishes, I ask Pamela what she notices from this one example.

"It's like a snapshot, isn't it?" she says. "First of all, this has a lot of numbers behind it, so it must be important. My first thought is that I have to continue with these particular meetings. But what if they all come out like that? Let's do more so I can compare."

We plot a few others together.

"I love doing this," says Pamela. "It took me a while to get the hang of it, but then it sails by. And what's most amazing is that as soon as I begin to plot an activity on this matrix, I know its value. I've never before taken the time to deconstruct what I'm doing this way. The analysis is immediate and frighteningly obvious."

Informal meetings							
Objectives	**Activities**						
	Office drop-ins	Telephone consults	Hallway encounters	Lunch dates			
A Increase market share	7						
B Develop direct reports	2, 3, 6						
C Build cross-functional systems	7						
D Position self for VP slot	7						
E Establish information networks	1, 2, 3, 5, 6						
Criteria: 1 Meets objective; 2 Personal enjoyment; 3 Learning opportunity; 4 Immediate application; 5 Long-term payoff; 6 Cannot be delegated; 7 Not applicable							

Professional development							
Objectives	**Activities**						
	On-site graduate marketing class	PowerPoint training workshop	Work with mentor	4-days-per-month leadership devlpmnt program	Work with coach		
A Increase market share	1, 3, 4, 5, 6						
B Develop direct reports	5						
C Build cross-functional systems	7						
D Position self for VP slot	1, 3, 4, 5, 6						
E Establish information networks	3, 5						
Criteria: 1 Meets objective; 2 Personal enjoyment; 3 Learning opportunity; 4 Immediate application; 5 Long-term payoff; 6 Cannot be delegated; 7 Not applicable							

Professional development							
Objectives	**Activities**						
	Develop marketing strategies, various projects	Create and monitor budgets	Collaborate with other departments	Work with IT to develop marketing systems	Provide ongoing feedback to direct reports		
A Increase market share	1, 2, 4, 5, 6						
B Develop direct reports	1, 3						
C Build cross-functional systems	7						
D Position self for VP slot	1, 3, 5, 6						
E Establish information networks	1, 4						
Criteria: 1 Meets objective; 2 Personal enjoyment; 3 Learning opportunity; 4 Immediate application; 5 Long-term payoff; 6 Cannot be delegated; 7 Not applicable							

At our next session, once Pamela has completed the matrix and had some time to consider what it can tell her about which activities are valuable to her and why, we look at some general issues, big and small, that the whole exercise seems to raise. One big issue that comes up repeatedly is delegation. At first, Pamela does not see the connection between paring down certain of her activities and developing others further. I ask her examine all of the #7, "not applicable," entries and explain why they aren't applicable. For example, she agrees that it would be a large stretch to see how her on-site graduate-level marketing class contributes anything to the building of organization-wide cross-functional systems.

On the other hand, with regard to the NMI team meetings activity, I want her to check her assumption that there is no opportunity here to develop the skills of her direct reports. At first Pamela says, "I *am* the meeting. What I mean is that I manage that team. There's just no way for me to step aside in order to develop someone else's skills."

"Do you assume that you'd have to step aside to bring someone in?"

"Marian, are you suggesting that I stay in place as the team leader but add another member to the team? Someone who might eventually take that role?"

I answer her question with one of my own. "How would that work? What might it accomplish?"

Pamela begins to think out loud. "I could bring Keesha onto that team. Her creative talents aren't really being exploited. She knows most of the members from other initiatives. She's never led a high-profile team, so this would be an opportunity for us to work on those skills while she watches me at first—we call it just-in-time training. I'd make it clear to everyone that I'm not stepping down or turning over any of my responsibilities right now, but that maybe someone else from the team might be ready to take over after a while. Then perhaps I could rotate off, with Keesha replacing me as our department representative."

I acknowledge Pamela's idea and briefly describe the delegation triangle checklist (*see* Chapter 8), which might help in any preparatory discussions with Keesha.

As Pamela continues to take a macro view of her matrix, she immediately sees both the waste of time represented by most of her unscheduled meetings and the redundancies in her professional development activities.

The latter is easy to clean up. Five activities produce the most "hits" with regard to her criteria, three of which focus on similar issues. She feels that right now she's getting the greatest immediate return on investment from having a coach; nice feedback for me. Initially the guidance provided by her mentor within the organization was very helpful, but while this person will continue to be a valuable resource for her—*and* she owes him a debt of gratitude—perhaps she doesn't need to spend as much time as she does checking in with him.

In the same vein, the leadership development program provides a wonderful platform for talking with peers and improving leadership skills, but Pamela has lots of peer exposure and at this point she feels that the skill development is happening faster in our one-on-one coaching sessions, so maybe it would be all right for her to drop the program as long as she explains why she's doing so. The on-site graduate marketing class, PowerPoint computer-training workshop, and coaching sessions will all end in a few months. Once that time is also freed up, Pamela can reassess the question of how to continue her professional development.

The unscheduled meetings—people dropping by, pulling her aside in the hall, or monopolizing her at lunchtime—are another story. She's made herself so available to people that they might not respond well to new behavior. We generate a list of actions that she could take to change the situation gradually:

❑ Kindly but firmly say, "I can talk for five minutes now, or would you like to schedule a half-hour meeting when my calendar permits?"

❑ Ask for the purpose and expectations of an informal meeting; if someone hasn't thought it through well enough to answer these questions, invite them to schedule an appointment when they have.

❑ Make lunch appointments rather than have them occur *ad hoc*.

❑ Send an email informing people of designated daily times (e.g., 8–9 a.m. and 4–5 p.m.) for informal, drop-in meetings—and explain why.

❑ Hang a "Do not disturb" sign outside your cubicle or office when you're working on a task requiring uninterrupted time.

❑ Forward all calls to voicemail and respond to them at designated daily times.

❑ Keep walking when someone buttonholes you in the hall and tell that person you can talk only as long as it takes to reach your destination.

❑ Hold ten-minute "water cooler" talks; let it be known that when you have ten unstructured minutes to spare you might be found at the coffee pot or water cooler.

❑ Put yourself on your own calendar; if you have a task to accomplish that previously would have gotten done at home, outside of work hours, schedule a time to do it at work instead.

❑ Have an all-hands meeting to tell everyone what you will be doing and why—from the heart—and to acknowledge that by changing your behavior you are asking them to change theirs as well.

❑ Above all else, stick with it.

Finally, I know from years of experience with many other people that it just isn't necessary consistently to work ridiculously long hours. So I tell Pamela to conduct a personal experiment: she should come to work a half-hour later and go home a half-hour earlier for two weeks and give herself a productivity review at the end of that time.

THE RESULTS

Two weeks later, Pamela tells me that not only does no one seem to notice the change in her hours, also she seems to be getting more work done during the shortened days. We concur that this might be due to the halo effect, so she should keep her eye on the topic for a while longer. Whatever we might call that effect, it has persisted since then.

She's also doing much better with the informal meetings. Merely telling people that there are expectations and boundaries has produced results; now when people drop by, they ask her if it's a good time to put a question or clarify an issue. The ratio of formal to informal meetings has changed too. Pamela shares her formal meeting schedule with others in the department and posts the times in the week that she's available for drop-ins. Those hours are controlled and specific. At first no one dropped in and that worried her, but eventually both Pamela and her colleagues figured out how to use these drop-in slots quite efficiently for quick consults and spur-of-the-moment updates.

One interesting byproduct of less accessibility to Pamela has been greater interdependence for all concerned. People who used to go immediately to her now go first to the person who is most directly responsible for a specific function or task. Information flows faster since she no longer has to be the clearing house.

I ask Pamela what the best result of her behavior change is.

She says that it's her ability to control her own time. "I still feel like I have more to do than I can accomplish. I accept that as a personality trait. What's different for me now is that while I still work hard, I enjoy it more. I'm no longer obsessed with what I don't accomplish and focus more on what I have achieved.

"Undoubtedly, my life is better balanced. My eleven-year-old and I made a cake together the other evening. When I asked him what the occasion was, he said it was a celebration of eating together as a family."

Getting hold of the way we spend our time is crucial at work and at home. We too often blame poor time management on others. There are the same number of minutes and hours in everyone's day, and for all of us it's crucial to use them wisely and well.

7

The Beginner's Mind for Old Dogs

SKILL: Customer outreach

TOOL: The beginner's mind

CLUES CATEGORIES: Underlying motives

Sometimes people get to be too good at what they do. They live in their "silo," lose touch with how they're viewed, and ignore their "customers" both inside and outside the organization.

The trio of finance managers in this story is rudely awakened by customer dissatisfaction within their company. We journey with them as the looking glass is reversed and they see themselves through the eyes of others.

THE SITUATION

The three finance directors of X Corporation, Inc.—Mary Sue, Trent, and Ranji, all of whom have worked for the company for at least seven years—have asked for help and I've been hired to give it to them. They've sent out a customer satisfaction survey to internal clients and have been shocked by the negative responses.

The top four issues revealed by the survey are slow delivery, not acting like business partners, displaying a condescending attitude, and lack of creativity.

THE APPROACH

The four of us sit down to talk about the meaning of each of these four issues. Mary Sue, the most senior person, tells us, "When I started here almost 14 years ago, we were told our job was to provide and analyze numbers. It was not to give advice. As the business has become more complex, I do help people understand the meaning of the numbers that I supply. But obviously that's not enough."

I chime in, right here at the beginning. "Let's see if we can unravel the messages. What was your reason for sending out the survey?"

Ranji replies, "Every department must do that once every two years. It's company policy. It's important that our customers, both internal and external, are happy with the level of service they receive."

"What kind of responses did you get two years ago?" I ask.

Mary Sue says that there were no negative messages and people seemed satisfied.

To determine what has happened over the intervening two-year period I suggest that we ask the customers directly. "Trying to second-guess meaning is dangerous," I tell the three members of the team. "We could go way off the path, developing and implementing ideas that come from our interpretation of words on paper. How do you think we could find out what's really behind all this negative feedback?"

Trent suggests that we develop an interview protocol and ask the same questions in person of at least two people in every "customer" division of the organization. "That means we'd have to talk to sixteen people, or five each. They've already spent a lot of time filling out the survey. To start with, I think we need to talk to the head of each department at some length. If someone doesn't feel able to speak for his entire department, then we can talk to another person in that department as well. Remember, we have our regular jobs to do. They'll *really* complain about our being slow if we spend too much time on this." Ranji's points seem to be heeded.

The three finance managers divide up the eight customer departments within the company and develop an interview protocol to ensure consistency. The protocol is simple and clear:

The purpose of this interview is to better understand the four major gaps identified from the Finance Department Survey. Please describe, in concrete terms, how each gap shows up in your daily interactions with Finance.

How do we demonstrate:

❑ slow delivery
❑ not acting like business partners
❑ displaying a condescending attitude
❑ lack of creativity

What would we be doing differently if we were satisfying your needs and wants?

The interview process is concluded in a week. When the trio convenes to report on their findings, Ranji begins.

"My three people are all new employees, young recruits fresh out of graduate school. They want a lot more raw data to pore over. One of the guys said he thinks we sanitize the numbers for them. One gal [Ranji is a bit out of date in terms of politically correct terminology] said that we act as though we're the only ones who can truly understand finance and we're much too territorial. She thinks every number in this company should be open to every employee. The third person commented that we're so slow because we won't let anything out until it's well packaged."

Mary Sue continues, "I had some similar remarks. On the good-news front, one guy said this is the first time in his tenure here that anyone from Finance bothered to ask his opinion. He said a lot more too—I guess he was making up for lost time. You asked that I include the CEO in my interviews. He thinks we should get out into the field more to rub elbows with the end customer. I wrote down his comment, 'It's easy to take pot shots at you because you're recluses. People can refer to and think of you as Finance and not *people* because they don't ever see your faces. I think half the complaints will go away if you walk out your doors.'"

Before the others can become defensive or dismissive, I speak up. "I see by your faces that you're not comfortable with that comment. Just let it sink in and we'll return to it after we've heard from Trent."

"Well," Trent says, "I talked to people who've been here even longer than we have. Pat over in Operations said we should teach everyone in this company, at least all the managers, to understand business financial basics. You know, profit, loss, margin, shareholder price, ROI—the basics, financial management 101."

"Why?"

"Pat said that people are uneducated about how this business runs. Or any other, for that matter. If more people understood the fundamentals, they could make better decisions and be less wasteful. Pat also said that we should be more visible. Let's see what else I wrote down here... Oh yeah. 'Finance is viewed as the exclusive club of eight snobby people.' That's not good."

"No it's not," sighs Mary Sue. Then she rallies. "Where we didn't get much help, in my opinion, is about what anyone means by lack of creativity. Creativity and finance are incompatible as far as I'm concerned. Look at the so-called creative accounting that's sunk so many businesses. I have no intention of letting that happen here. Maybe they mean they'd like our reports to look more like they do in USA *Today*. You know, colorful graphs and charts with sidebar commentary."

It takes several hours for all of the interview results to be discussed. I keep reminding the group to stay open-minded and to look for patterns and themes in the comments.

No matter how good a job they're doing at not being defensive, they don't seem to have any idea how to look at the information that might be gleaned from the survey and the interviews through the eyes of their customers. I want to come up with an approach that will allow them to look freshly *at* Finance instead of *from* it.

I suspect that a powerful underlying motive is at work here: fear of being outsourced. There's a very real possibility that if internal customers are dissatisfied with their service, the company might go outside to hire an independent firm to replace the whole Finance Department. So for this corporate team, building better relationships with customers is crucial.

THE APPLICATION

The Beginner's Mind is a simple and powerful concept: Return to the time when something was new; see things like a child exposed daily to new information and challenges; enter an experience without prejudgment or knowledge. As a learning tool it may not lend itself to every situation, but it is useful when people are stuck in old ways of thinking.

I propose a two-step approach. First, I explain the Beginner's Mind and ask for examples of such experiences in people's lives. Mary Sue talks about watching her grandbaby, who's a beginner at everything. Ranji reminisces about leaving India and starting anew as an adult in London, and Trent recounts how learning to play golf humbled him.

To keep this Beginner's Mind experience work related, I ask if they'd be willing to do what their CEO suggested, rub elbows with their customers. They're willing, but they want more details.

I offer to cook up something with Pat in Operations.

Pat and the Human Resources people—aka HR—decide that the trio should go through the company's hiring and orientation process. "I bet they'll be shocked at how hard it is to get a job and start working here," she says.

All three are eager to do it. And it's not easy, either. First they have to write and submit their resumés. Ranji has to provide a contact from his university in India because HR isn't familiar with the school. ("It's the premier finance and economics university, I'll have you know!" Ranji says indignantly. But he complies nevertheless.) Trent's resumé isn't in a standard format, so he has to make many changes. Mary Sue's looks "light" because she's only worked for two companies since she graduated from college.

They sail through the hiring interviews because no one other than the CEO challenges them.

Still, filling in the second round of papers for HR is daunting. Mary Sue complains about all the legal information and Trent bridles at being put on as a contract worker for a trial period. They actually take the three-hour orientation program and are weighed down with a huge binder full of procedures, contact information, policies, and forms. "By the end of the first hour my head was swimming," Ranji says when we all meet together again.

"So what did you learn?" I ask with a smile.

"I can't believe what we put people through," Mary Sue says. "There has to be a faster, easier, more involving way to grasp all of this information. Here we are in the computer age and mostly everything was given to us on paper—reams and reams of it. I felt like a passive player in a very complex and intricate process." She sounds disgruntled.

"And what feedback would you give HR?"

"Come of age—use technology. Look at new hires as customers, not potted plants. Tell people the reasons for your policies, not just the end results."

"Does any of this strike you as familiar?" I ask.

Trent's face shows his awareness. "Oh-oh. Did you know the orientation process was so much like what our own customers complain about?"

"Absolutely not. My goal was to put you through a Beginner's Mind experience. Let's assume it's coincidental that your words echoed those of your own customers. What are your thoughts about that?"

Trent is the first to volunteer. "Both our procedures and those of HR are focused on *our* needs, the needs of the department, not the needs of the user. It's very clear to me that HR is much too concerned with legalities and procedures and too little concerned with making new employees feel welcome. In Finance we collect the data we need, put it through our mill and spew it out, without ever involving the customer in designing the process or the presentation format."

"That might be the case, but how do we know?" asks Mary Sue.

"Good thought, Mary Sue. Testing your observations is the second part of the approach."

"Right, I forget there were two steps. What's next?" They are all eager to delve further.

This is a good time for me to press. "If you hadn't been compelled by the company to conduct a customer satisfaction survey, would you have done one?"

Ranji speaks for the group. "If you'd asked that question two weeks ago, I think we would have said no. But now that we're in the throes of getting to the bottom of how we're perceived, we're grateful that the survey turned up potentially dangerous signs."

"So what are your actual motives, now, for learning from your customers?" I ask.

"I guess we've been operating as though there are no problems," Trent says. He's getting closer. "We just wanted confirmation that we were doing well, like in the past. But the business climate has changed so radically and quickly that no department can afford to bury its head in the sand."

"But what's your basic concern or fear?"

Mary Sue takes a stab at saying what's hard to say. "We're motivated to keep our jobs. Underlying our interest in talking to customers, experiencing the Beginner's Mind, and trying to figure out a way to improve our service is the possibility that our function, Finance, could be outsourced. We'd be out of jobs and it seems our customers wouldn't care. We've got to beef up our quality, speed, and service."

Silence follows, and head nodding. All three people look stricken. Bringing their unspoken fears out in the open is a challenge as well as a relief.

"So," I propose, "now that you have a feel for the Beginner's Mind, let's follow one of your own key reports through the collection, analysis, and dissemination process. Do you think you can do that through a novice's lens instead of from the standpoint of being the experts that you are?"

They decide to follow the infamous hours report that's done by Finance bi-weekly. On Friday of every second week, the managers of each of the company's departments send Finance the number of hours worked by all employees under their supervision. Finance calculates the cost per department and for the entire company. It takes a pro rata figure for salaried employees and uses actual costs for hourlies. That cost is compared to orders, margin, budgets, and projected overtime.

A software program generates the report itself. Nevertheless, it takes two full days for a data-entry clerk to input the information and run the numbers. The report is then reviewed by Mary Sue and distributed back to the other managers on Thursday of the next week.

The next time the appointed Friday comes around, Mary Sue, Trent, and Ranji sit at the elbows of managers who are filling in their forms. They learn that most managers spend an extra two hours at the end of the day on this task—not a popular one. It's also apparent that some of the numbers are likely to be approximate because it's hard to determine exactly how many hours a salaried employee works. "I tell guys to jot it down at the end of every day, but they forget," says one department head. "They're thinking of getting home after being here for ten hours. Plus they think the report is silly."

Each of the Finance trio also sits for a few hours to watch the data-entry clerk. Ranji says that he's bleary-eyed after two hours and comments, "I wonder how accurate the entry process is after he's been doing it for two days in a row."

Once the data from all the managers cycles through Finance's computer, Mary Sue spends all of Wednesday morning reviewing the individual reports on each department before they are printed and ready for distribution.

Continuing to follow the process, they hand deliver the reports this time, to find out what the department managers actually do with them. In every case, the report is barely scanned and quickly filed. In addition, Mary Sue learns that the CEO only looks at one of every two reports. "There's nothing to be gleaned on a bi-weekly basis," he says. "Once a month is enough for me to be able to see trends."

The team, now fully engaged from a Beginner's Mind point of view, wonders about the origins of the report. Trent goes back to his three interviewees because they've been with the company the longest. Lo and behold, one person says that she thinks these bi-weekly department reports were started in response to a lawsuit about ten years ago. "All of a sudden we had to keep track of everyone's hours because one employee accused the company of paying salaried workers overtime instead of using hourly workers. That doesn't make much sense, does it?"

"Nope, but I'll check it out." Trent is able to discover that the first hours report was in fact generated about ten years ago, as his source speculated. He even called the retiree who was the head of Finance at that time, who told Trent that the then CEO wanted the report to "keep salaried employees in line," to let them know that their time was being watched as carefully as that of workers being paid by the hour.

Following these revelations, Mary Sue sits down with the current CEO and asks if the report has any value after all. He's never heard the story about the lawsuit, but he thinks it's funny. "Pretty bogus, huh?" he laughs. "But getting a single consolidated monthly report on the cost of hourly work by department is still helpful. And I also need to keep track of the ratio of contract workers to salaried employees, so we don't end up in trouble with the government. Is there a software program that can produce a report like that?"

"Absolutely." Mary Sue feels a little relieved. "We have it already. Boy, will people be thrilled by *this* change."

"OK, let's work on it," the CEO says. Then, "What else will Finance do to be more customer focused?"

"We're going to meet with new employees, especially ones fresh out of graduate school, to ask what kind of raw data they actually do want and how they'd use it. They all have jobs to do and so do we. We want to provide information that makes their jobs easier; but on the other hand, we don't want everyone to establish their own mini-Finance Department." Mary Sue pauses.

"I'd also like to put together an advisory committee of new and long-term employees," she continues, "to help us see our work through their eyes. This all comes out of an approach Marian taught us, the Beginner's Mind. It's really altered our perspective, and we think the company will benefit if we keep on with it."

THE RESULTS

Three very crucial changes have come about within this company as a result of the Finance team thinking like a beginner:

❏ Five of the Finance Department's routine reports cr report cycles have been scrapped, combined, or significantly modified.
❏ All department heads take an on-site, custom-designed, eight-week finance fundamentals course.
❏ A finance advisory board has been established, and each senior Finance team member sees at least two in-company "customers" a month to discuss business issues and their financial implications.

Since a small incident can sometimes be emblematic of a larger change, I can report that the last time I was in the company cafeteria I saw Mary Sue sitting at lunch with someone from outside her own department. They were exchanging photos of their grandchildren.

Energy

8

Buried Alive

SKILL: Delegation

TOOL: Delegation triangle checklist

CLUES CATEGORIES: Energy, Stories, Characteristics

Capable people often have a difficult time with delegation. The litany goes something like this: It's not a good return on investment for my time, complex work is dangerous to let go, customers expect my personal attention, and work that reaches my desk belongs there.

Nevertheless, it just isn't possible to accomplish all of the tasks brought before an executive single-handedly, so knowing how to delegate, when, and to whom is a critical managerial competency.

This story is about an executive whose lack of delegation skills almost derailed her career.

THE SITUATION

Howard, the executive vice-president of finance in a pharmaceutical company and a former coaching client, calls me to talk about Ernesta, one of his direct reports. "Ernesta has very high potential," he says. "She's just been promoted to director level after only three years and already has the attention of our executive committee. She's a brilliant analyst with degrees in theoretical mathematics, an MBA in finance, and a PhD in economics. She's moved up quite rapidly in the organization.

"I see her as a CEO some day, but she's going to be derailed if she doesn't work more efficiently with people. She takes on more and more, doesn't let go of work, and stays longer hours than anyone else. I tell her to go home, delegate work, take a day off, and use her vacation. I'm not subtle. Look, I'm concerned that she'll have a breakdown if she doesn't come up for air."

"What in particular has gotten you so alarmed?" I ask. "You sound pretty concerned."

"I suspect that there are nights when she doesn't go home. Last week I noticed her scurrying out of her office when I came to work earlier than usual. I thought that she was wearing the same outfit as the day before and she was carrying a little bag. A little later she reappeared in different clothes and with damp hair. I didn't want to confront her, but that kind of behavior upsets me when there's no reason for it."

"Was there a major project that might have required her attention?"

"No," says Howard. "Sure, we're swamped, but then we always are. It's not possible to work enough to get to the bottom of our piles."

"Howard, does Ernesta know that you're talking to me?" He mumbles a yes. "What did you tell her?" I ask.

"I told her that you were my coach and that you helped me with my meeting management skills. I offered to ask you to work with her about work–life priorities. I don't think she would have sought out someone like you by herself, but she seems genuinely happy at the prospect of having a coach."

THE APPROACH

I call Ernesta and she says that the only window she has open is two days from now at 8 a.m. When I express surprise about the fact that she keeps her own calendar even though she has an assistant, she offers, "Oh, but I couldn't expect anyone else to understand how I choose to spend my time."

When I arrive at Ernesta's office she's talking on the phone in French. She hangs up, comes to the office door, smiles broadly at me, and shakes my hand vigorously. I'm surprised by her presentation. She's wearing a bright red dress (no wonder Howard recalled what she was wearing if this attire is any indication of her usual wardrobe), a lot of expensive-looking jewelry, tasteful makeup, and has highly styled copper-colored hair. She's tall, about 5'10", and statuesque. Ernesta tells me that she's excited about having a coach and isn't at all threatened by it. "I want to be a superb leader," she blurts out. I notice a slight accent, definitely western European.

In the limited time we have together I ask Ernesta what she wants from a coach. I explain the coaching process and inquire about her work experience. Then I ask what she perceives to be her greatest challenge. Without any hesitation she replies, "The amount of work I have to accomplish. Even though I can do more than 90 percent of the people in this company, I can't seem to make a dent. And I realize I can't be impatient with people who can't think and take action as fast as I can, but sometimes it's hard not to be."

"How do you think you come across to people? What do you imagine people say about you?" I ask with genuine curiosity.

Ernesta laughs a little and comments, "I think I'm a puzzle to most people. I dress up every day because people expect finance heads to be dowdy. Fortunately, this is a sophisticated global company, so the fact that I'm a polyglot of nationalities myself doesn't matter. You know, being able to speak five languages is not freakish in Europe like it is in the States." She pauses. "Probably the most often heard remark about me would be 'She works hard.' I do. I work long hours, I'm thorough, and I'm available."

She has certainly given some thought to the image she projects.

"Let me go out and check with other people to see if they agree with you," I suggest. "Is that all right with you?"

"Yes, Marian," she says immediately, "by all means. You have access to anybody. Go ask what it is like to work with me. Go ask them what I do well, what I do poorly, what I should do better. I want to hear this. Do it in person, too. I don't want one of those anonymous pencil assessments. They'll say more in a conversation."

Together we craft a few questions and select a cross-section of people to interview. I want to make sure we get a well-rounded picture of Ernesta.

Everyone on the list is willing to talk. One person says, "I'm not sure I can explain how my boss acts. She's a very complicated lady. I'll sure be glad to try though."

It takes me two weeks to interview everyone. Their collective portrait of Ernesta shows that she's regarded as being highly intelligent, able to see right through a problem, calm under stress, creative in the way she crafts solutions, sensitive to people, and genuinely nice.

On the flip side, another picture emerges, one of a person who works at a breakneck pace, takes on any work thrown her way, and doesn't let go of a task. No sooner does one project get started than she hurls another at the team she supervises without clarifying its relative importance. One person who works closely with her says, "I feel like I'm a crab working to dig my hole in the sand. Every so often a tidal wave comes over me and I don't know what's happened or what to do. And I have to check to see if I'm still alive."

As an aside, another direct report says, "What do you make of those outfits she wears? She comes in looking like she's working for a fashion magazine and acts like only the bottom line matters. It sure is an odd mixture."

I also want to know what her department's internal customers have to say. Repeatedly I hear that not enough work gets done even though Ernesta and her direct reports are very capable. Projects stay in her office too long, so that by the stage when others get involved time and their ability to add value have been wasted, and sometimes her in-company clients feel cheated. Nonfinancial people in particular feel inadequate because Ernesta thinks so fast and never explains just what it is that she's thinking.

I see three or four issues here: project organization and prioritization, boundary setting, clarity and frequency of communication, and that old conundrum, delegation. I'm not going to touch the wardrobe.

Choosing the skill that offers the greatest leverage, I decide to focus on delegation. In most cases I engage the client in setting the direction of the coaching, but Ernesta's crunch of time pushes me to skip ahead. Besides, if she improves her delegation skills, this will have a positive impact in other areas. For example, she'll have to be better organized and put work into priority order merely to identify what work to delegate.

As I think about what specific tools or exercises to propose, I hearken back to Ernesta's office and our interactions to look for clues. There are some clear signals: models and flow charts on the office whiteboards, her request for data from my interviews, and her reference to finance as a complex system. These clues about process and structure, plus the general consensus that Ernesta seems driven, lead me to revise a model I've used previously. I believe that she'll resonate with a concrete, visual, and systematic way of viewing delegation. If she can grasp it intellectually, then she'll be more open to changing her behavior and language.

We meet and I raise the topic of delegation. "What does that really mean?" Ernesta asks. "Who is to assume it's a good thing anyway? I give my people work, isn't that delegation?"

I don't rise to the debate, but we do talk about the term. We discuss why anyone would delegate work to another person, what circumstances make it easier or more difficult to delegate, and how people differ in their desire and ability to accept responsibility. Eventually Ernesta says, "I want to know how to delegate and to whom. I can handle that. It's clear and straightforward."

"To get us started then, describe the delegation process you currently use."

Ernesta thinks for a while, eyes closed, and begins, "All right. I look at the complexity of the project. If it's too difficult to explain or if I'm not sure if anyone's ever tackled anything like it before, I keep it. If a project can be broken into segments, I divvy it up and spread it around to the best resources. If it lies within someone else's area of expertise, I meet with that person and give it away. Also, it depends on whom the work is for. Some people's work just can't be done by anyone else but me because I've always handled their work."

I decide not to challenge that last assumption quite yet.

We continue examining Ernesta's current delegation practices. Finally, after we can see her patterns and explanations, I tell her I'd like to show her a model I use that might guide her approach to delegation. For the next few minutes can she mostly listen while I explain some materials I've prepared for her? She nods.

"All right," I begin, presenting the first sheet, a simple little chart. "Let's think about delegation as a triangle. One leg of the triangle is *To do*, the other is *Can do*, and the third is *Will do*. If you're going to delegate to somebody effectively, you must pay attention to all three sides of the triangle.

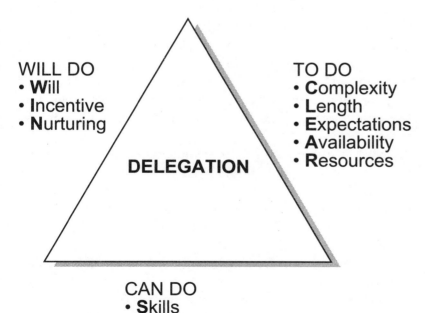

WILL DO
• **W**ill
• **I**ncentive
• **N**urturing

TO DO
• **C**omplexity
• **L**ength
• **E**xpectations
• **A**vailability
• **R**esources

DELEGATION

CAN DO
• **S**kills
• **E**xperience
• **T**raining

WILL DO
• Will
• Incentive
• Nurturing

DELEGATION

TO DO
• Complexity
• Length
• Expectations
• Availability
• Resources

CAN DO
• Skills
• Experience
• Training

"To do is the task. That is, what is to be done. To grasp all of the aspects of this side of the triangle, use the acronym CLEAR. For someone to do what is required, the parameters of the task must first be made clear." I give her my itemized list of the elements behind the acronym.

"The words behind CLEAR are Complexity, Length, Expectations, Availability, and Resources.

"To determine the *Complexity* of the task you must analyze how many pieces there are, what the interdependencies are, how sophisticated the knowledge required to solve it is, and what precedents exist. Is the task simple, somewhat complicated, or very complex?

"The next part of CLEAR is *Length*. How long do you think it's going to take to do this? If you determine that it is a very complex task that's going to take months to do, the field of delegation candidates will narrow. If it's a simple, quick task, the field may be wider.

"The third letter is *Expectations*—your expectations. Excellent problem solvers often start with the end in mind. Clearly state what success is and what it will look like. I can't tell you the number of times I hear about projects that failed because people went off in a different direction than the delegator intended. And the worst part is that people tell me they don't have time to talk about expectations upfront. A huge amount of time is saved when people are aligned from the start. If you can't explain the desired results, you won't get them.

"Next is *Available*. Do you, the delegator, have time available to coach the person or people you're entrusting with a task, and do they have time available to be coached? I think it's unfair, even unethical, to delegate if you don't build in time for feedback and consultation. You'd only be setting the whole process up for failure.

"And finally we have *Resources*. Are there appropriate resources to support the person to whom you're delegating? Too few resources can sabotage the process because too much time is spent scratching for nutrients. Conversely, too many or the wrong resources can be overwhelming or may be misapplied. How often do you delegate a project without the necessary resources of time, people, information, and technology to do what is required?"

I note that Ernesta is listening attentively and making notes. I ask for her thoughts about the model so far.

"I can see already that I'm in trouble," she says. "I've always believed that the person I delegate to should be able to take the task and run with very little direction. I can operate with very little guidance, and now I realize that I expect the same from others. I always provide a list of resources, but I've never thought to put myself on it."

We talk about how her preferences might not mirror the preferences or skills of people in her department. "Could you successfully accomplish any task you were given during your first few years of work?" I ask.

She responds, "Of course not, but I figured out how to do what I was given without asking for much help. But OK, it's possible that my recollection is colored. I might have needed more help than I realize." She tells me to continue.

"Once you've established that the To do is CLEAR, you move to Can do or Will do. It doesn't matter which comes next. Let's go to Can do."

This side of the triangle also has its own list of elements. "The framework follows the acronym SET: Skills, Experience, and Training. They're pretty obvious. Does the person have the technical and personal *Skills*, prior *Experience*, and access to *Training* to accomplish the task? If the person lacks any of the three, he or she isn't SET. Then you've got to find a vehicle like training, a class, coach, or mentor to make up the deficits." I sit back to indicate that I'd like to hear Ernesta's reactions to this part of the model.

"You know, Marian," she says, "I'm embarrassed to admit it, but I think people aren't very bright if they don't know how to do what I ask them to. We pride ourselves on hiring very smart employees, but sometimes, frankly, it doesn't seem that way. Book smart and work smart are different. Tell me about the third side, then I want to talk about the whole thing."

"The third side of the triangle is Will do and the acronym for what it involves is WIN: Will, Incentive, and Nurturing. Personally, I think this is the most challenging part of

WILL DO
• **Will**
• **Incentive**
• **Nurturing**

DELEGATION

TO DO
• Complexity
• Length
• Expectations
• Availability
• Resources

CAN DO
• Skills
• Experience
• Training

delegation. You've really got to know people to be able to delegate to their strengths.

"A leader needs to be able to ferret out whether a given person has the *Will*—the desire, curiosity, fortitude, commitment—to do what's necessary to accomplish a given task. I'm wondering if you're sometimes confusing people's will with their intelligence. That is, you believe that being smart is equal to having the will to tackle something difficult."

"Ooh, that's a potent notion." I can see Ernesta reflecting on this distinction, so I press on.

"Figuring out a person's *Incentive*—what's in it for me—takes real interpersonal skill." I pause. "Ernesta, not everyone in your organization wants to be you. Everyone doesn't operate like you do. Do you know what drives your direct reports? And here's a clue, it isn't money first."

Ernesta thinks for a nanosecond and comes up with, "Sure, everyone wants to learn new skills, get better performance reviews, move up the ladder."

I add one more possible motive. "How about getting more decision-making authority?"

"Actually," she says, "I've never given much thought to what incentives drive my folks."

I can't let this one go. "Well, Ernesta, before you look to them, can you answer that question for yourself?"

Ernesta smiles and says, "I was afraid you'd ask. Sure, there are those that I declare publicly, like being an inveterate learner and wanting to do a superb job. But there are others that I don't like to acknowledge."

"Such as?"

"I love going to Wall Street in my high-fashion clothes and running circles around that condescending club. I like the game of trying to outthink the competition. And I'm very seduced by money and power."

I point out to Ernesta that she spoke the first, publicly acknowledged list in a very calm, soft, controlled voice. The second—her declaration of unspoken, underlying motives—was said loudly, with passion and without equivocation.

She interjects, "I wonder if I don't delegate much because I don't want people to see that competitive second part of me.

I feel safest working alone or performing for a group. I don't feel comfortable working one-on-one or with only a couple of people."

"That's an important insight. I wonder if having a delegation model to fall back on will make any difference to you?"

"Why don't you finish explaining the model," she says. "Then I'll practice over the next couple of days. The only way I'll know if it's useful is if I apply it. By the way, could you stay around while I do that?"

"Sure." I go on with the last bit of the model. "The final letter in the WIN acronym stands for *Nurturing*. That is, will the person being delegated to feel secure enough to take a risk? Is he or she being developed before, during, and after the learning process? I would have hated to learn how to ride a bike by being thrown on to one and told to ride. The hand of my big brother on the back of the seat was the support I needed to feel confident enough to listen to his instructions as he ran alongside. Isn't that what you're asking for from me? Stay around and support me while I learn a new skill? That's just what your direct reports want too."

THE RESULTS

Ernesta decides that she'd like to turn the model into a checklist (I actually have one prepared, the delegation triangle checklist in Part II, but I don't want to spoil her sense of discovery).

Because everyone in her department knows that I'm coaching Ernesta on her delegation skills, I'm invited to sit in on several handoff meetings over the next few days. I explain that my role is to be a silent observer, not a player in the interaction.

The first meeting, with a woman named Sonja, is tense. Neither side quite knows what to expect. I sense that they feel as though they're auditioning for a role in a movie. Ernesta hands Sonja the checklist and tells her that it might be easier to follow along if they're both working from the same piece of paper (two actors with one script).

This gesture produces immediate results. Sonja gets the gist of the model right away and seizes the opportunity. "Here, in CLEAR, you've approximated the length to be about five to six weeks," she says. "That doesn't seem to jibe with the resources piece. Part of that time I'll be in Brussels, so we'll need to find a way for the two other projects I'm in charge of to be covered when I'm out of the country." And, "My expectations are that I can have access to the market study analysts and you'll be available to show me which ones are most relevant."

When the two finish their hour-long delegation session both remark how valuable it was.

Ernesta closes the door and mutters, "I felt like screaming in there. It took so *long*, and Sonja asked so many questions."

I retort, "Then why did you tell Sonja that the time was well spent?"

"Because I could see that she was liking the process. I didn't want ruin the attempt."

"So what are you going to do now?"

"Well," says Ernesta, "I have another session scheduled this afternoon. I'm going to go through with it because it might be different than this one with Sonja. Maybe I'll take a relaxation pill first."

"Is that the best way to deal with your frustration? And what do you intend to do about Sonja?" I ask in a very calm voice.

"Nothing. We've made an agreement and I'll live up to it. Goodness, do you think I'd throw away all that precious time I just invested? I know how to handle frustration, you watch me. I'll be perfectly professional and patient with Philippe."

Ernesta's attitude bothers me. I certainly don't want her to behave as though she's doing this for me, nor do I want her to approach it as a game. In any event, I'm off to a nice restaurant for lunch, alone.

The meeting later that afternoon is definitely different. I guess that Philippe has talked with Sonja; he seems to come prepared to challenge Ernesta. She follows the same protocol of giving the checklist. When they begin talking about the complexity of the task, Philippe says, "You and I have different views about the complexity issue. You say that the task involves knowledge of international rulings; therefore you want to oversee that part of the project. To me it's not so complex. In my last job I dealt with international courts of law all of the time. Why can't you trust me to proceed? I don't need your oversight."

I observe how flustered Ernesta is. I want her so badly to follow up with a question instead of arguing with Philippe. There's silence in the room. Ernesta takes a deep breath and says, "All right, you can have it. So, I guess if you're so sure of yourself, we don't need to go through the rest of this list."

Philippe looks shocked. "Ernesta, I thought this meeting was to help me be able to take on a task that you're going to delegate to me. Sonja said that her meeting with you this morning was great. If I can't question your thinking, the situation will be the same as always. This checklist won't do any good if we can't discuss all the items on it. You've got to trust in my ability. Otherwise, I don't want to work here."

Now it's Ernesta's turn to look shocked. "Are you thinking of leaving?" she asks. "I don't want you to go."

"Is that because you want me and my skills or is it because you don't want to have to recruit someone new?"

"That's pretty harsh, Philippe. Of course I'd like you to remain in the department." This is hard for Ernesta. "I'm sorry I flew off the handle. This is new to me and I'll be honest with you, I'm not comfortable."

"That's obvious. I have nothing to lose here, so I'll be frank. Ernesta, you're brilliant. I took this job to work for you, but you're not *letting* me work for you. You're your own department and the rest of us orbit around you. I'm smart and I have a lot of excellent experience that you can tap into. I want to be a part of your department. Don't waste me."

The silence that follows is a bit awkward. Then Ernesta rallies. "Whew. Thank you for being so candid. Do you want to proceed, or should we take a breather?"

Philippe plows on. "Can we continue through the checklist? I always thought that you were so cool and impenetrable. Thanks for getting riled—it's easier to work with you as a real person." They work together for about 45 minutes more, going through all the points on the list.

By the time Philippe leaves, Ernesta looks exhausted. "No wonder I don't like to delegate," she says. "That checklist seems like some sort of torture mechanism. It gives people permission to talk about every item on it until they're satisfied. It's draining... But I think that Philippe was courageous to say what he did."

She chooses to hold another delegation meeting the next day. This time at the end she says, "That was one of the nicest meetings I've ever held. Haeyoung liked very much sitting down with me, seeing the triangle, and negotiating the steps. Something happened between yesterday and today. It's strange, but I feel relieved. I have more confidence in my folks and I feel more connected to them."

The fourth and last meeting I witness takes a surprise turn. As Greg and Ernesta talk through the checklist he says, "I think this is a nice project. But you're talking about something that's too long and complicated for me, with the skills I have now. I like my job, the kind of work I do, and the amount of time I can spend with my family. It would cost the company some money to give me more training, and it would take a lot of time for me to get up the learning curve. Thanks for the opportunity, but I don't want to do it."

Ernesta thanks Greg for his candor and assures him that his response won't hinder his job security in her department. Later she says to me, "Well, talk about Will do. You and I will have to work on how to motivate people like Greg. But for now, I'm relieved that someone said no. I'm not sure it's realistic to assume that every case will end with a clean handoff.

"I like the model," she adds. "It gives me a crutch to use until I learn to be instinctive about delegating to people. I also think that it helps me open the door to talking with people in a nonthreatening, objective way. I need to determine if the time spent on delegation is time well spent, but that will take a while to know. You and I have other issues to deal with, but I'm feeling good about where we are on this one. Thanks."

Ernesta's experience in learning to delegate is like learning to drive in a new, strange territory—albeit with a map. When she's got the model in front of her she can negotiate anything that comes her way. When she fails to think through a project or tries to wing the conversation, she gets flustered and reverts to old patterns of behavior.

Nevertheless, there are two strong indications of change.

First, customers write emails saying how grateful they are for the speed and quality with which finance projects are getting completed. Ernesta shares every note with her whole department and that results in a visibly more cheerful departmental atmosphere.

Second, Ernesta takes a vacation. She goes on a two-week cycling trip through France and calls in to the office just once a day. The department hums along well in her absence.

She also brings me a superb bottle of wine from a vineyard owned by family friends.

9

Hear Ye, Hear Me

SKILL: Brainstorming

TOOL: "Write, speak, post" brainstorming

CLUES CATEGORIES: Energy, Language

*B*rainstorming, which *Merriam Webster's Collegiate Dictionary* defines as "a group problem-solving technique that involves the spontaneous contribution of ideas from all members of the group," was popularized in the 1950s by Alex Osborn. It can be a most valuable process in all kinds of contexts, but it is also widely misunderstood and therefore not always well implemented.

When I work with teams I often ask if they use brainstorming as a method for generating ideas and solving problems. If they do, I ask under what conditions and with what guidelines. Then I watch a brainstorming session to see how they use this technique and if there are ways to improve its effectiveness for them—which is often the case.

This is a story about a team with a double challenge: Its members come from many parts of the world and so traditional North American-style brainstorming will be abnormal for some; in addition, no one on the team really knows what the key elements of the process are.

THE SITUATION

The president of a transportation company has put together a truly global group, with representation from Canada, Chile, Egypt, France, Japan, Mexico, Poland, and the US. What this carefully selected team recommends will have worldwide impact and it's crucial that everyone's thinking be heard. I've been hired to help ensure that happens.

Typically, brainstorming is implemented by gathering people together in a fairly comfortable place, presenting them with broad issues or questions, and encouraging a fast flow of comments and ideas that are recorded on a flipchart or whiteboard for further consideration. A key element of this process is that all members of the group feel free to participate: The basic premise is that any one of them may come up with a suggestion or insight that solves a problem or points to the best course of action for the future.

In this case, however, by the third team meeting I observe mostly lopsided brainstorming. That is, only the people who are quite fluent in English join in the fray. The others say very little and look uncomfortable. They face away from the flipchart at the front of the room, clear their throats before speaking, make no eye contact, talk in low tones, and sit up poker straight.

THE APPROACH

On the spot I decide that this group needs guidelines for brainstorming that will enable everyone to participate on a more equal footing.

"We've spent time talking about how you like to think, learn, and participate," I tell them. "We've also talked about how cultural differences influence the way you think and behave. Well, for the past 15 minutes I've seen you struggle with brainstorming, and I think maybe the way you're working is not accommodating stylistic and cultural differences. Does that ring true for you?"

The man from Egypt is first to speak. "Absolutely. The ideas from certain folks come so fast that I can't find a way to add my responses."

"I like to gather my thoughts before speaking," says the woman from Japan.

"Funny," says the Canadian who volunteered to be the scribe, "I wondered why a couple of people didn't look at the chart while I was writing down the ideas."

Other comments reinforce my observation and speak to the discomfort that some in the group have been feeling. We listen to them all.

"So do you have another idea, Marian?" asks the representative from Poland.

I think carefully about how to accommodate the different backgrounds and styles of the group's members before I respond.

"Let's try something new," I suggest. "You'll still be brainstorming, but with a modification to the process.

"I'll give each person a pad of sticky notes. When you have an idea about the topic, write it down—one idea per note— then speak the idea so that everyone can hear it. Then hand the notes to me and I'll post them on a chart. What do you all think of that approach?"

From the Canadian scribe: "I like the fact that we can all put up ideas as they come. I found it frustrating to have to be writing on the flipchart while I was trying to come up with my own ideas."

"But I still may not be able to give you all my ideas so fast because I have to write in English," says the Japanese delegate.

"That's a very valid point," I say, and it reminds me of another important aspect of brainstorming. "This is not a contest to see who can come up with the most ideas. Our purpose is to get your *best* ideas. Would you prefer to write in Japanese, then translate later?"

She smiles. "It takes a lot of characters to make a word. I like that option, though. Let me see what works out best."

Then we hear from the Chilean. "Won't it slow us down to write, say what we write, and then post the ideas? Why can't we just write, then post? What's the value of saying our ideas out loud in between?"

"Another good question." I am beginning to form a reply when the American delegate picks it up.

"The biggest benefit of brainstorming," he says, "is adding to one another's ideas. If I don't hear your idea, I won't be able to add to it."

Most people nod in agreement.

THE APPLICATION

"So," I say. "Do you want to try? If it doesn't work, we can stop." More nods. There is consensus.

"All right then. Let's try this new method on the question 'What do we already know about the region?'" At first there is confusion. Some people blurt out their ideas then write them, others write and forget to speak, and some forget to hand over their sticky notes to post.

I keep reminding people to pay attention to all three steps by chanting, "Write, speak, post." And I make encouraging, nonevaluative comments as they give me their pages to post on the chart ("You're coming up with a lot of ideas," "What an impressive list," "You're building off each other," "Thank you").

Gradually everyone gets the hang of the write, speak, post tool. They begin to slow down, take time to write, and clearly speak the entire idea. And far more ideas are generated than emerged in any previous brainstorming session.

When it appears that the group is finished for the day, I ask how they liked using this modification of the brainstorming process. It receives rave reviews. Everyone likes the relative anonymity of contributing their thoughts in writing. Someone comments that hearing me say "Write, speak, post," was soothing and encouraging. They all like being thanked for their ideas. To a person, they are amazed at the number of ideas that have been posted on the flipchart sheets.

I ask for their theories about why they came up with such a large quantity of ideas.

"Lack of time pressure," says one.

"I really listened to ideas, thinking time was OK—I could come up with an idea in my language and translate it in my head without feeling like I was fumbling," says another.

"It felt like a game," comments a third. "The way you eagerly took our ideas and posted them. And you know, I don't think we actually once commented on an idea. There was truly no judging. We were caught up in the process."

THE RESULTS

Over the next weeks the team members doggedly practice "write, speak, post" brainstorming. I urge them to change groups, seats, tables, and location in the room continuously. Every time someone picks up and moves there is a fresh perspective.

Many members of the team tell me that they like this modified approach to brainstorming so much that they are committed to taking it back to their home bases to teach to others.

Stories

10

Ideas, Fresh and Delicious

SKILL: Metaphorical thinking

TOOL: Visual essay and metaphorical thinking

CLUES CATEGORIES: Stories, Energy

Many of our most creative ideas bubble up from internal sources over which we have relatively little conscious control. First something stimulates the mind, and then it incubates below the surface until the moment of "aha!" arrives. That's why it is sometimes hard to create on demand—there's no time to let our brain go through its subliminal idea-generation process.

For example, an artist might be commissioned to produce a piece of original work with no boundaries set for what it should look like or even what it should communicate, or be asked to render an interpretation of a specific idea or place. A scientist might want to develop a drug to treat a particular disease or be assigned to model a certain protein. Each of these is an example of how a catalyst—general or more narrowly focused—begins the mind's churning.

Creativity is important in the business world as well, from big ideas about products and services to small suggestions about the workplace that might have a significant impact on a company's operations and productivity.

This story is about a team charged with developing a new product. Its members are hampered, however, by their company's previous successes, and they need a fresh way of accessing original ideas.

THE SITUATION

"Hello, Marian, do you have 15 minutes for me to explain our situation?" I'm fielding a call at a prearranged time from a potential client.

"Shoot."

"We're a confection company. I'll tell you our name later, if we get that far. It's time for us to introduce a new product, but we don't have one in the pipeline. Sure, we can make incremental improvements to any of our well-known brands, but that's not what we're looking for here."

The caller, who turns out to be Harold Franken, vice-president of new product development for a company that I'll call Taste Brands, tells the tale of an organization that continues to rest on its 80-year-old laurels. Taste Brands was founded by a brother and sister who used their Swiss grandmother's recipes to make small, rich confections. The heirs of the company like to say that if the price of those little gems were to be adjusted for today's economy, each piece would be sold for nearly six dollars.

Taste Brands has evolved from the homemade days and is now best known for its international mini-bars. Some of these are the Danish Crispy Delight, Saudi Sweet Honey, Asian Fruities, Mexican Cocoa Chew, and American Mash Bar.

"Some of our food sells well in certain areas and not in others. We're hoping to create a new confection with a global appeal so we can centralize our marketing and cross geographic boundaries."

After a few more discussions, I agree to act as a coach/consultant to help the product development team as they work toward this new goal.

Right away, during the first session I spend getting to know the team, it's obvious to me that they're in a rut. Their body

language speaks of a lack of energy. Almost everyone has a coffee mug in hand, heads are angled downward, people file toward their usual seats at a series of tables in the large conference room, and there's a serious lack of banter.

I ask what's on the table so far.

"We have ideas," the team's spokesperson of the day says, "but they're still regional. Like a French-Twisted Straw—you know, to put into coffee. Or how about Icelandic Icicles made of spun sugar to look just like icicles?" Clearly these are the kinds of ideas they've come up with before. "That's not what Harold wants, though."

He's right about that.

THE APPROACH

This gang is in need of a jolt far greater than sugar or caffeine can provide.

Usually when I conduct breakthrough thinking seminars, I wrest the participants away from their problem by taking them on an excursion to get a fresh perspective. What would be best for this company, I wonder. A mall? No, too reminiscent of life as routine. Children's museum? No, they'd probably be too uncomfortable. I'd like them to stretch but not break.

Here it is: It's a big group, and that may be part of the problem. So I'll divide them up arbitrarily—stir up the mix—and give each smaller team a more thematic assignment, one that they'll have to decide how to fulfill.

"How ready are you all to engage in some serious and fun idea preparation?" I ask. "Preparation is the first phase of the creative process, like the pieces of grit in the oyster shell. Few of us can create on demand. We need something to stimulate our consciousness to begin to think of original ideas. Are you game?"

One voice speaks for them all. "If you can help us come up with what Howard wants, sure."

"I won't do anything that compromises my ethics or values," says another of the team members.

I quickly assuage their worries on that topic.

Just suggesting that we're going to do something perks them up. I notice smiles, a few elbow jabs, and attentive stances.

"All right. Here's the drill. There are 18 of you, so let's divide into four groups. I suggest that we choose the groups by birthdates. That is, the first quarter will be in one group, the second in another, and so forth. Do it by month and day, not year. Then rearrange yourselves around the tables accordingly." There's laughter and a couple of people wonder out loud if this is an experiment to test the validity of birth signs.

I'm glad to see how willing they are to be brought out of their daze.

"Please choose one person at each table to be that table's emissary. Emissaries, you'll pick a card from the hat. On the card is your group's assigned topic. So the rest of you, if you don't immediately warm to your topic, blame the emissary."

I make this little joke with a smile; it's to reduce resistance to the topic. And before they even get their assignments they join in the mood: "OK, emissary—our fate is in your hands." "Hey, Frank, your bonus is riding on what you pick out of that hat."

In the "hat" are the following topics:

❑ Children at play
❑ Adults at leisure
❑ Seniors with hobbies
❑ Teens hanging out
❑ Preteens shopping
❑ Baby boomers working

I've purposely put in more topics than there are teams because even though this is essentially a lottery, I don't want the last team to feel as though there are no choices.

Each team also gets a sheet with instructions:

❑ At 1 p.m. the day after tomorrow you will present a visual essay about the group identified on the card that you selected.
❑ The essay is to tell a story about that group and how its members engage in the activity listed.

❏ Your presentation may not exceed 15 minutes.

❏ To complete this assignment you may choose either a video or disposable camera. Simply go to Camera Mart across the street to pick up your selection. The approval number to use is R685. If you already have a digital camera at your disposal, you may use it.

❏ Of course, I will be available as a coaching resource throughout the process.

They ask if they must work as a team, if the entire essay must come from the photos or videotape, whether they will be reimbursed for out-of-pocket expenses, and if the company lawyer will be at hand in case they are arrested for intrusion. I tell them that they will be reimbursed for reasonable expenses, to use good judgment, and to enjoy the process. The rest is up to them.

THE APPLICATION

They do a terrific and enthusiastic job. There are two photo essays, one digital, and one video variously on adults at leisure, seniors with hobbies, teens hanging out, and baby boomers working.

The video of teens hanging out is accompanied by music selected and edited by the teenage daughter of one of that group's members. "She really got involved. Without her there'd be no music and no real close look at teens. I think Angelina's a budding filmmaker," says the girl's very proud mother.

After each presentation the other participants write on charts the messages they've gotten from the essay they've just seen. The "baby boomers at work" list includes:

busy, intense, focused; bombarded with sound and visual stimuli; in the workplace, poor lighting, cramped quarters, papers everywhere, wastebaskets full, lots of motion; photos abound—of family, hobbies, vacations, co-workers—along with signs of achievement—awards, trophies, diplomas; people eat at their desks (snacks of fruit or chips or raisin packets, they snack most in late morning and afternoon) and look very tired as the day wears on; not much exercise during working hours; on phones and computers a lot; interactions are at meetings and coffee/water stands; people pop into one another's offices for quick questions/connections; personal calls are made throughout day, and takeout menus are posted on bulletin boards.

There's certainly a lot to think about here, and each essay generates its own equally amorphous list. We compare lists and look for themes and patterns, some of which are specific to a particular age group; others cross all groups.

"What words about food come up?" I ask.

We use the "write, speak, post" brainstorming tool described in Chapter 9 and they generate a list of 87 descriptive words. I congratulate them on their fine effort and suggest we quit for the day, but not without a parting shot.

"Let your minds wallow in subconscious incubation," I say. "Before you go to sleep tonight, write these words on a piece of paper, 'Ideas for a new confection.' Put the paper and a pen nearby so that you can capture any ideas as they float into consciousness. Don't edit what appears, just make uncensored notes. Bring that paper with you tomorrow."

"What happens if I don't think of anything?" a woman asks from the back of the room.

"This isn't a test," I assure her and everyone else. "It's an opportunity to get out of the way of your conscious mind. Let's see what happens."

When we gather the next morning, some people can hardly wait to talk about what happened to them during the night.

"I made this drawing around 4 a.m.," says one man. "I have no recollection of making it." His sketch shows children eating and growing, eating and growing, and each growth spurt is marked by bigger muscles and rosier cheeks. One person has only the phrase "Bite Time" on her page. Someone else has bunches of words: "natural ingredients," "local grains," "not dry." And another person has written, "Back to our origins—individual, distinctive, carefully made."

Other folks are quiet and puzzled about why nothing has popped up for them. I suggest it's likely that fragments of ideas will surface for them as well if they continue the practice for a while.

To make this point more directly, I tell a story about myself. I used to think that I didn't dream. However, since—based on what virtually every psychologist will tell you—that couldn't be true, I signed up for a dream workshop for which I knew the participants would be asked to record three dreams to bring along to each session. A week before the workshop began I put a notebook and pen by my bed. The first night I slept poorly— it must have been performance anxiety, I say, and the comment gets an appreciative laugh. The second night I awoke aware of unconnected images and stories still bouncing around my head. By the fifth night I could remember my dreams quite vividly, retaining good detail of sometimes as many as four different dreams in one night.

Armed with the idea that there are still more possibilities out there, we begin the process of convergence or coming together. At first people keep working together in their original groups, then we meet all together to evaluate the results.

At my suggestion, each team selects four images that best represent their essay. Next its members write words that resonate with each photo. For example, the "adults at leisure" team selects a photo of a couple playing tennis accompanied by the words " fit," "energetic," "educated," "time-bound."

Next I ask the participants of each group to visualize themselves as the people in the four photos, one photo at a time. They are to imagine their food preferences and dislikes and record them. They repeat this process for each of the four photos.

"OK," I begin when we gather together again. "Now you've identified the members of your mega-audience and their purchasing criteria. And in the process, of course, you've begun your marketing and advertising plan. All we've got left is to decide what the confection itself will be."

At this point, instead of conducting a large-group brainstorming session, I divide all the new product development people into three fresh groups. I want them to break out of the mindset that parallels the consumer group that they've just represented. Also, I find that mixing people together in new configurations usually increases the diversity of thinking.

THE RESULTS

Two weeks later, Harold comes in for the whole group's presentation of the members' recommendations. First they show a video of their target audience (included are pictures of the two consumer groups not originally picked by the "emissaries"), with descriptive words superimposed.

Then they give Harold a beautifully decorated soft box about the size of a jumbo candy bar. On top of the box are a photo of a hiker and the words "Bite Time." Strewn across the image are other words: "high-energy," "natural ingredients," "quick," "yummy," and "variety." Other boxes stacked nearby bear photos representing other consumer group categories: a teenager polishing a car, a school kid carrying a knapsack and a hockey stick, a couple playing golf, a wheelchair racer, two elderly women walking arm in arm, and so forth.

Inside the Bite Time boxes are several individually wrapped, bite-sized mounds that look like the first candies made by Taste Brands. Each of these is a different color and flavor, filled with different ingredients. Imprinted on the insides of the box are the story of Taste Brand's Swiss tradition; the company's philosophy; information on ingredients and nutrients, including how long it takes the average adult to metabolize a single Bite Time; and information about how to contact the company as well as a pulloff feedback card. Also there's an offer: A customer can send in three box labels to get a free Bite Time travel pouch.

Harold is ecstatic. He reviews the concept, financials, and market. He thanks everyone profusely, guarantees his support for the product, and tells everyone to take the rest of the day off (it's 10.30 a.m. on a Thursday).

Bite Time has done well. The travel pouch offer served as an excellent source of market research, enabling the company to track which images are the most effective, the age of the buyer, and how the pouch will be used. The fact that nutritional information was provided inside the box became a huge selling point and was written up in health, lifestyle, and parenting magazines. After six months, the company went on to

introduce a new line of Bite Time boxes, each filled with only one of the four different "bites." (There's now a Slo-Release Energy Box, a Fast-Burst Box, a Protein Pop Box, and a Sustainable Carbs Box.) These immediately found their own market niches.

From my standpoint, however, I still cared most about what would happen to the "new idea" department's ability to sustain its creativity. I used some of the ideas from my Thought Expanders® CD to jumpstart their creative processes—to pull out of their hats whenever malaise sets in. Here they are, some for individuals, others for groups or organizations:

❑ Organize a group excursion to a museum, zoo, park, or local college; or to play miniature golf or go river rafting.
❑ Go to work via different routes. (One person who had never ridden on a public bus in her life decided to try it—she had to get a schedule and routing, be at the stop at the right time, change buses, and walk two blocks at the end. It was quite an eye-opener for her in more ways than one.)
❑ Dress in an unusual style on dress-down Friday. (One man previously thought of as conservative showed up in a toreador suit.)
❑ Prepare a picnic in winter and find a venue where it can truly be a picnic.
❑ Bring in artists to demonstrate what they do and let people experiment with the media they offer. (This led one person to return to a love of writing poetry.)
❑ Sponsor (or attend) a lecture series, to be given by local university professors, on a topic or topics other than business.
❑ Go on a walking tour of the historical district of your town.
❑ Search for something arcane on the internet.
❑ Use the opposite hand for certain tasks for at least one week (shave, brush hair, switch watch, eat, pick up paper, play sports).
❑ Create a corner in the workplace for jigsaw puzzles, games, children's books, and an easel.

Obviously, this list is just a start—the idea is to do something new or in a new way, to get those creative ideas percolating.

Periodically I check in with the team members to see how they are doing. Harold has them working on ways to leverage the success of Bite Time. They take field trips to re-energize their thinking and claim to continue to generate very innovative ideas.

To me the team thinks of itself as highly successful, creative, and adding value. That mind shift is the real payoff.

11

Will the Real Problem Please Stand Up?

SKILL: Defining the real problem

TOOLS: The talking stick and Storytelling

CLUES CATEGORIES: Stories, Characteristics

We'd all be rich if we had a dollar for every time a group misdiagnoses a situation from the start and sets out to solve the wrong problem. All too often, a bias toward speed and immediate action outweighs thoughtfulness and discipline, and the result is costly in time, resources, money, and organizational effectiveness. Chronic problems abound in many organizations merely because sufficient time is not spent early on to define a problem properly, break it down into its component parts, and address each part carefully.

This is the story of a team struggling to break through the walls of past assumptions to find a solution to an ongoing and very expensive problem. Its members lacked a methodology to identify the separate issues with which they were dealing, let alone to generate fresh ideas to resolve a complicated situation.

I'm never surprised when a potential client says something like this over the phone: "We're a bunch of engineers sinking millions of dollars into a problem that we keep approaching the same way. I'd like to talk to you about helping us come up with some new ideas. We're afraid that management will shut down our operation because the cost-to-benefit ratio is way out of whack."

As Terry Granger, the client and project manager in this case, explains his particular situation, I notice that he talks mostly about his team's lack of creativity. He seems unaware that other factors, such as problem-solving skills, team interaction, or technical acumen, might play a role in their being stuck. However, I don't want to make any assumptions and after three phone calls we concur that I should spend two days with the senior members of the project team.

Terry understands that I'm not an engineer and have no content expertise. I wonder what he expects. I have an uneasy feeling that he believes I hold some magic secret that, when revealed, will solve the whole problem in a flash.

THE SITUATION

On the first day of this initial consultation I meet a core team of four people recruited from all over the company to focus on the problem of how to mine ore profitably from a vein lying partially beneath the edge of a town. Terry, the project manager I've spoken with before, is a very reserved chemical engineer whose previous experience has been mostly with oil rather than ore. Manfred (known as Man, never Manny or Fred) is a physical chemist and wants me to know that he is on the project because he is widely held to be the most creative thinker in the entire company. Micky is a young, rather flip mechanical engineer, and Trix (her given name, she insists) is a structural engineer who has earned her stripes by being smart and unintimidated.

I watch them in action for a day and make some notes:

❑ The team has been together for only three months.
❑ Informal roles seem defined already: Man throws out ideas; Trix asks questions and rarely says if she agrees or

disagrees; Terry talks only about facts and waits until almost the end of a discussion to enter; Micky cracks jokes and talks like he just came from a lecture on the subject at hand. There is no sense of cohesion.

❑ Each person talks from an unshared but often quite opinionated mindset.

❑ Most of the talk is circular. There's no structure or discipline to the thinking or discussion process.

❑ People seem to wait for Man to talk, although Terry is the designated project leader.

❑ Often the flow of talk goes like this: Man to Trix, Trix to Man, Man to the group, Micky to Terry, no response, Micky to Trix, Trix to Man, Man to the group, Terry to no one. They have definitely fallen into a communication rut that cripples their ability to be innovative.

❑ When a conflict of ideas arises, they don't know what to do, so Micky makes a joke and the conflict is diffused without being dealt with.

❑ Biggest "aha!" for me: They don't know what problem they're trying to solve. They behave as if this was a brand new situation. I wonder who else has been involved in the past.

I have stipulated that I will need to talk individually with the team members to ask a few questions, so I'm scheduled for one hour with each, plus an hour with the company vice-president who brought this crew together. I want to talk to him first, to put the others in context.

Mike Matthews, the VP, is a hardy-looking man in his 50s who peers intently at you when he talks and speaks emphatically. His whole manner implies that he's rarely content to sit in his office. Mike has been with the mining company for his entire career and his office is decorated with photos of mines from many locations. He points them out and tells me, "I've worked in each one of these, I'm proud to say."

I inquire about the team, how and why each member was picked, and the goal for the project.

"Well, is this confidential?" he asks. "I need to be able to trust that what I say will not be betrayed."

I assure Mike that confidentiality comes up in every coaching assignment, and that I have a pristine record in that department.

"OK. Let's start with Terry. He's a deep vein of gold. He's delivered on every project in his career, doesn't ruffle any feathers, and is extremely smart. I chose him to lead this team because he's got the patience to hang in for the long term and won't try to run over anyone in the process. My concern is about his decision-making abilities—he doesn't like to come down hard on nonsense. Terry and I conferred on asking you to come in to work with us, and he favored the idea because he thinks the project will be de-funded if we keep going the same old way. Terry's usually right. He's a good guy who wears well."

"What do you mean by 'he doesn't like to come down hard on nonsense?'" I ask.

"To answer that I have to talk about Manfred. I don't call him Man. Manfred sees himself as the idea guy. Actually, he's more about stirring up the pot. This is one of the things I need you to keep confidential. Manfred was assigned to this project—I didn't select him. My boss said that if I wanted to take a stab at leading the project, I had to take Manfred too. If you ask me, Manfred gets so wrapped up in his own ideas that he doesn't think about their practicality. But hey, maybe that's just what this project needs. You keep Manfred on target; get him to think about what will actually work, and we'll be pals. I don't think Terry will do that."

"Go on," I say, indicating that I've heard his opinion without necessarily endorsing it.

"I wanted Trix and Micky for their expertise. Trix is a first-rate engineer. Also she knows some of the folks in the town that's built over the vein. And Micky is with us as a developmental assignment. He's fresh out of graduate school, but he's interned with us for a few summers. He brings new thinking into the project and he knows he could get another job in a day, so I don't think he'll be afraid to say what he thinks."

We talk more about the team, Mike's reasons for hiring me, and his goals. I don't learn much more than I already know, but I do believe that Mike will be supportive of the work I do with the team.

"Is that it, Marian?" he asks.

"I have one more question about the project. How many people over the years have worked on this same situation? And where are they now?"

"Jeez," Mike pauses to think. "I'd say about a dozen to twenty. I'd have to sit down and make a list. Probably about half are still working for us. Why do you ask?"

"Well, I'm thinking about having all those folks in for a talking session. This current team is new to the issue. Why take the time and resources for them to learn what the others may already know? What do you think? Could we do that?"

"Hmmm. You're here to help us come up with new ideas. Won't we just get bogged down in old thinking?" Mike's resistance to this idea doesn't surprise me. I've been here before.

"I'd like to get everyone together," I say, "to share history, experience, success, failures, ideas that weren't ever tried, what the barriers were. If we can hear everyone's stories, we'll have a shared pool of knowledge to draw from. If these people are going to come up with breakthrough thinking, they have to know what they're breaking through."

Now it makes sense to him. "Got it," Mike says. Then, thoughtfully, "Actually, I'd love to sit in on that session. I've never heard the whole story myself. I'll round them all up. Do you want retired people too?"

"Yes, everyone who's touched the situation; anyone who has a story to tell. How long do you think it'll take?"

"You're talking to an action man. How about two weeks from yesterday?"

"Terrific," I tell him. "I'll design a protocol for the day." But I also need to let him know that there's a great deal more to be done.

"There's a bit more, Mike. This team needs me to coach them on how to work together. They don't seem to know how. And they have no method for solving problems. Frankly, I don't think they'll come up with anything new or different without some guidance about the process." I pause to let this sink in. "I'd like to work with them regularly for the next six months."

After we talk briefly about scheduling and how this might unfold, Mike agrees.

"All right. We've sunk so much money into the ground, a little on the surface won't hurt." I smile at his metaphor. "Send me a bill for your services—just don't be wasteful. And are you sure you want to spend six months with these characters?"

THE APPROACH

One thing for sure, I decide, I will use the Talking Stick with such a large, diverse, and opinionated group. I had used this device before, but without much understanding of its true origins. Then, shortly before taking on this assignment, I had met an American Indian tribal elder who told me about the practice among his people.

"First of all, the Talking Stick is a substitute for the person holding the stick. So the stick itself must be beautiful and ceremonial. And in order for it to work it must be respected. Everyone has to recognize the power and place of the stick.

"The person who brings the stick to the group—you in your work—must bring a special stick. So you, Marian, must go out into the woods and say a prayer, sing, dance, or meditate. When you sense that you are ready, walk around until you spy a stick that asks you to pick it up. Hold the stick, listen to it, talk to it, really feel it, and when you are certain that you belong together, bring it out of the woods and into your home.

"Wash the stick the way you would wash your body. Make it clean and smooth, but don't pull off any bark that is stuck— that bark belongs there.

"Then decorate the stick in any way that pleases you. At one end, make a place for the stick to be held. I usually wrap that end with material so it will feel nice to hold. My stick also has feathers, beads, seeds, and shells. Take time to make it personal.

"Tell people that the Talking Stick must be used well. Have everyone sit in a circle and demonstrate to them how to accept, hold, and pass the stick. The stick must be offered; it cannot be taken. So when a person finishes talking, he or she holds the material-adorned end toward the body and points the other end of the stick to the center of the circle. When the spirit moves another person to talk, he or she stands up and takes the offered stick, talks as long as is necessary, then offers the stick to the room.

"Tribal belief is that when the stick is talking, everyone else is listening. Actually, the elder doesn't speak in a talking circle. We say he is a leader because he has been chosen to listen."

I thanked my adviser and have done my best to honor his teaching ever since.

Mike lives up to his promise and two weeks later delivers 16 people for a one-day talking circle. My goal is for them to define the problem that the core team is currently facing.

There are thirteen men and three women, including Trix. The men look more like extras in an old western movie than attendees at a business meeting. Almost everyone is wearing some form of blue jeans and boots, there isn't a button-down shirt in the room, and many of the faces I see are lined by the sun and wind.

Mike and Terry stand before the group, whose members are already making snide remarks about their chairs being arranged in a circle. Mike begins.

"Thanks for being here today. As is our usual tradition, we'll supply you with all the lousy coffee and stale donuts you can stand. In turn, we want to hear what you have to say. This gathering was the idea of our coach, Marian Thier. So if it doesn't work out, blame her. I'm going to introduce the project manager, Terry Granger, to you. Terry will introduce the team that's assigned to Vein 66. It's this team that we hope you'll be helping."

Terry introduces the core team and turns the meeting over to me.

I also thank everyone for being willing to be a part of this experiment. One of the fellows says, "Anything to avoid another day of retirement golf is a relief." There's lots of good-natured ribbing of the retirees. I ask everyone to introduce themselves and briefly explain their involvement with Vein 66. From what they say, I can tell that there's a lot of history and experience in the room.

I explain the concept and use of the Talking Stick—my first risk with the group. To my surprise, one participant is a Native American and he tells the group that my explanation is accurate. He makes one addition, however. "You can speak more than once," he says. "A talking circle isn't considered successful, though, unless every tribal member speaks at least once. So don't hog and don't stay out."

I show everyone the six steps we'll follow for the day. I also admit that I have no idea how long the process will take because this is the first time I'm using it. A couple of them joke that they'll participate until drinks arrive.

THE APPLICATION

In addition to the Talking Stick, we're using the standard tools for a brainstorming session: big sheets of white paper taped to the walls, for writing outlines and ideas on, and sticky notes for quick additions and organizing. I've outlined some steps to help structure the discussion.

STEP 1: RECEIVE PROBLEM

Step 1 I've labeled privately "Receive a partially cooked problem." For public consumption it's just "Step 1."

Terry hands out a one-page summary of his group's understanding of the situation with regard to Vein 66. It's written clearly and factually, like any good engineering problem. There is much head shaking. A few people begin to grab for the Talking Stick. I ask them to wait until we move into Step 2, which is coming right up.

"All I'd like you to do in Step 1," I tell the group, "is read the summary and ask Terry questions to clarify what is written. For example, you might want to know how dollars were figured, or when something occurred. But this isn't the time for debate or opinions."

There are a few specific questions. The ones that can't be answered get posted on a "parking lot" section of wall.

STEP 2: TELL YOUR STORY

"OK. Now jot down some thoughts. Soon you're going to be talking about your relationship to this problem. But before you begin to talk, take a few minutes to make some notes about what you want to say. As we said in the letter Mike sent you, we want you each to tell us about how you fit into the story of Vein 66. No solutions or blaming. Imagine you're sitting in a rocking chair on a porch, cold beer in hand, telling a brand-new Vein 66 recruit about what you did there and what you know.

"The purpose of this step," I continue, "is to create a shared understanding about the problem or situation. Here are a few guidelines to follow that should make the stories flow and add to a cumulative body of knowledge."

The guidelines are written on the board:

❑ One person at a time speaks without any interruptions (remember the Talking Stick).
❑ Each person adds to what has previously been said, without repeats.
❑ Begin your story with the word "and" (you are building an encyclopedia).
❑ Do not go in any preconceived order, speak when your additions seem most appropriate.
❑ Talk about what you know: the project's history, your involvement and experiences, the contributions of other people—good, bad, and ugly.
❑ Speak the truth—as only you know it.

I pause for questions, then add, "You can jot down key words or questions that pop up, but don't take notes—stay with the stories as they unfold."

The first person to pick up the Talking Stick is one of the retirees. He tells about going to the site for the first time. The company had purchased the rights to the vein and brought in a corps of engineers to prepare it for mining. Much to everyone's surprise at the time, there was evidence that this site had been mined before. "I guess the engineers who did the due diligence survey didn't probe far enough," he comments.

Everyone sits quietly, in rapt attention, listening to his story about the earliest days of the company's involvement with Vein 66. When he finishes, it takes a while before someone reaches for the stick to begin another story.

"And my job was at headquarters, around the same time. I was responsible for working with the Bureau of Mines. What a challenge that was. They were crusading to clean up mines that were eroding the land and fouling the water. They just about shut us down before we could conduct our own tests."

The younger engineers and scientists make no attempt to interrupt as a very complex chronology of events and circumstances unfolds.

After about two hours, Trix takes the stick.

"I don't hear much talk about the folks who live in that town," she says. "My parents did. They left when my dad retired from the mine. One day my dad was driving along when a pothole opened and his car sank so deep it looked like the car was being buried. Another time everyone on our block got sick from something that leached into the water. Yeah, the state fixed that pothole and we sealed the leak; but it's a losing battle for the people who live over the vein."

There's an uncomfortable silence in the room. The men respect Trix, but she's speaking of a harsh reality that few in the company want to face.

Something amazing happens with Trix's story, though: Everyone in the room begins to speak much more authentically. Their stories do not all have happy endings, nor do they testify to accomplishments and successes. Instead, people talk about their fears and frustrations: waste, accidents, data that was ignored, politics, poor decisions, the failure of good technology.

We break for lunch at 1 p.m., after everyone has told his or her story. I ask if they have the stamina to continue.

"We're all wound up and ready to go," is the consensus. "As long as these cheapskates give us a good lunch."

"The purpose of this step," I begin after our break, "is to identify patterns and themes that have surfaced in the stories that people told this morning. To do that, please divide into groups of three."

STEP 3: IDENTIFY ASPECTS OF THE PROBLEM

"Should we arrange ourselves according to similar jobs or by chronology?" someone asks.

"That's a good distinction." This person has raised the point that I was about to make. "It seems to me that the best configuration would be of unlike trios. That way you're more likely to see different aspects of the problem.

"There are three parts to this assignment," I continue. "First, talk with one another about what you heard in those superb stories.

"Second, consider both patterns and themes that surfaced for you. For example, themes might be 'Our equipment always lags behind state-of-the-art' or 'We have the best mining engineers in the world in our company' or 'No one confronts the issue of the people living above the vein' or 'We make changes without talking about why we're changing.'

"Third, write one pattern or theme per sticky note—use the felt pens and sticky notes that I've distributed about the room. Then post your stickies on the wall.

"What you're doing," I explain, "is like pulling out each strand of spaghetti from a huge bowl of steaming pasta. After you're finished posting your work, walk around to read everyone's entries."

The trios talk, write, talk, write, and then post. I notice that most groups wait until all of their ideas are down on stickies before they post them. By the end, there are two walls full of patterns and themes.

Before I can suggest that trios ask one another for clarification, they're already doing it.

"Hey, Thompson," says one of a threesome, "I saw you put up this section. What do you mean by 'TGIF syndrome'?" Thompson walks over to tell them his answer.

It's taken only about 45 minutes, until 3 p.m. or so, to complete Step 3. I see that people are beginning to flag and I also know that cocktails are scheduled for 6 p.m. I suggest a coffee break. Mostly people grab a cup and continue to talk about the ideas on the wall, so I move them right along.

STEP 4: COMBINE ASPECTS OF THE PROBLEM

"The purpose of this step is to display the patterns and themes in clusters. This should go pretty quickly.

"First, combine repeated ideas. Don't just discard repeats, because later the number of repeats might weight the importance of those ideas. Keep them together in a cluster.

Then make larger clusters for ideas that seem similar. And, finally, add a title for each cluster."

People break into small groups to discuss how to arrange the wall. I stay out of it. I notice that not everyone participates in this step. When I check in with those who aren't participating, they say that there are enough people milling about. However, no one seems annoyed.

It takes this rather large group only 25 minutes to cluster and label almost 200 ideas. I commend them for their speed and ask those who did not get to cluster to verify the choices that have been made. There's agreement on the five clusters: information about the vein itself, equipment, engineering, the town, and project management.

STEP 5: WRITING THE NEW PROBLEM STATEMENT

It's now 3.30 p.m., but everyone wants to continue so I press on with the next item on my outline: "The purpose of this step is to write problem statements for each of the identified clusters."

I tell them that writing a strong and comprehensive statement of the problem is the trickiest part of problem solving. If the problem statement doesn't invite innovative thinking, the best one can hope for is an incrementally improved solution. I also suggest that the group members develop their own criteria for the problem statement. These will help them focus on what future efforts should include.

The criteria that they develop are:

❑ Is breakthrough thinking possible?
❑ Will it be worthy of the resources that are to be spent?
❑ Will the solution make a difference?
❑ Is there passion in the organization for the point of view?
❑ Can it be achieved?

Next I introduce the concept of a "How might we" (HMW) problem statement. I tell them to begin each problem statement with "How might we…," a phrase that's invitational and open. I immediately receive a lot of positive reactions to thinking about a problem in that way.

Together we work on one of the five clusters—the vein itself—to practice writing problem statements. After only about ten minutes the group comes up with: "How might we remove ore without weakening the infrastructure of the vein?", "How might we mine only the richest areas of the vein?" and "How might we shore up already mined parts of the vein?"

Someone says, "We'll have more than a dozen problem statements if we go at this rate. How will we choose which ones to pursue?"

Another person interjects, "You mean, 'How might we choose the right problem to work on?'"

We all laugh and I point out, "That's why we didn't discard the repeats on the wall and why we developed criteria. We'll use a multi-vote in the next step to come to agreement on the critical few."

They break into groups of five to write problem statements for the remaining clusters. All day long, at my suggestion, they've been shuffling groups to prevent the iron grip of "groupthink" and remain open to the energy offered by considering different perspectives. They finish this part of the process, proud but tired, at 4.30 p.m. There are 16 problem statements.

STEP 6: MULTI-VOTING FOR THE CRITICAL FEW

"The purpose of this step," I announce when they tell me they want to keep on, "is to choose which problem statements will meet your criteria."

I provide them with the details of multi-voting:

❑ Total the number of problem statements (16).
❑ Divide that by 5 (roughly the number of people in each group at this point), which is (approximately) 3.
❑ Each person will get three dots to be used to vote. Voting is based on the established criteria. That is, which problem statement(s) do you believe best meets the criteria?
❑ Dots can be placed on one, or two, or three problem statements—that is, each person's vote can be spread around or focused on one problem statement.
❑ The problem statements with the greatest number of votes will be the first to be addressed.

It is clear that everyone takes this seriously. People read the statements over and over, without the usual chatting and bantering. They pause to ask for clarification if the wording of a statement is not absolutely clear. Tentatively at first, they move forward and place their dots. It does not appear that anyone changes their mind according to who else votes for which statement.

There are three clear "winners" and several others close behind. Only a few problem statements receive no votes at all. The one with the most votes is the one we developed together: "How might we remove ore without weakening the infrastructure of the vein?" The second is about the town: "How might we meet the needs of the town while continuing our operation?" And the third comes from the "geology" category: "How might we use the shale structure as an asset instead of as a barrier?"

Everyone wants to know what's next. Immediately, to quell doubts, I say, "The core team and I will meet in the morning to talk about how to assess these statements and move along these lines. We'll have an outline of the next steps by the end of the day tomorrow. How's that?"

There are nods but no more questions.

"Before we break for drinks, I'd like you to indulge me one more time. Please write on stickies anything you want the team to know, think about, or do. And sign your name, so they can get back to you. Also, to help me learn to do my own job better, write down a couple of your reactions to this day—what worked and didn't work. How you feel now about the process. You can put them right here." I indicate a corner of the last suggestion sheet.

"OK," I then say to end this very long and successful day. "Let's give ourselves a big pat on the back. You guys did yeoman's work today. I so appreciate your willingness to hang in there with energy."

THE RESULTS

Terry and Mike (the latter, by the way, intended to stay only for the storytelling but never left) are profuse in their thanks to the participants.

Mike says, "If only we'd taken this kind of time to reflect and organize our thinking years ago, we wouldn't need to be here today. But we are here and you have my word that we'll move forward."

Terry ends with, "Hey, if any of you want to be on a problem-solving team, let one of us know. Obviously there is a lot of brainpower in this clan. And you'll get coached in the process."

In the quiet of my hotel room, where I flop exhausted from the day, I read the final comments that I asked for from members of the group. Even the greatest skeptics have something good to say. The "didn't work" comments are mostly about time; in particular, several people suggest the process be conducted in two half-days because "one day is very intense" and "it's hard to stay focused for so long." My favorite among the comments is "I forgot how stimulating work can be."

The next morning I meet with the members of the core team to ask for their reactions. Trix, uncharacteristically, speaks first.

"I had no idea that so many people have feelings of guilt about the town. The fact that one of the final problem statements is about protecting the residents shocks the socks off me. I want to head up the group that works on that issue. I've never been so invigorated, so determined in my career."

Immediately Man jumps in. "We could move residents away from the vein. How about getting the Bureau of Mines involved? Why not work with a local developer?" I put up my hand. (If I am careful and aware, I can often use my status as an outsider to get someone to reconsider his or her habits and tendencies.)

"Man, those are interesting ideas, and they're premature. Right now I need everyone to stay on track. We're talking about yesterday." I can see him switch gears as others almost sigh with relief because I've redirected another brainstorming excursion back to the point at hand.

Basically, everyone agrees that the day was worthwhile. Then Terry asks a leading question. "OK, we've restructured our thinking about the problem and have a clear mandate to move forward. But how are we going to do it all? We're only four people—who, by the way, have work responsibilities beyond this project."

It's Micky who answers. "I know it feels overwhelming to think that the four of us can solve a problem that's been around for years. But I'm sure that we can develop a good, sound project plan. Once we do that we'll go back to Mike and present our case—with facts to support it."

From Terry, "You know, over drinks last night several people said they'd be interested in working with us. I got their names. But Marian, what's your part in this?"

They've already come a long way, I tell them. With the help of the veterans, they've made great strides in identifying the elements of the Vein 66 problem. But in order to find new and viable solutions, they'll need to change certain habits of thought and interaction.

"One issue," I say, "is the way you work together as a team. Like any team of people, you have strengths and weaknesses. My guess is that you're not particularly aware of either." Some glances and a nod tell me that they agree. "Mike wants me to continue to work with you to practice your strengths and change weak behaviors."

Everyone wants to know what I've observed already. I tell them something of what I've written in my notes, which fascinates them. Trix says, "I feel like you're an intelligent TV camera." I don't disagree.

Terry wants to know if I'll be with them every time they meet. "I have to submit a budget to Mike," I say. "Tell me what you think would be helpful to you."

They feel that I should be there to observe and consult solidly for the first two weeks, half-time for the next six, then once a week until they make their final recommendations.

"I want to put a six-month cap on my time with you, and for the project," I reply. "If we don't begin with an end in mind, we won't work as diligently as we will if we have a deadline."

I tell them that there will also be time for individual coaching—that's the third element of the consultation that I've discussed with Mike Matthews. "I'm aware that this is a team effort. Nevertheless, each of you has a career that requires individual performance at a high level. I will spend an hour every other week with each of you, either in person or on the phone. We'll address your leadership challenges and skills, personal work agendas, and issues for which you want a sounding board."

Trix says, "Already you've made a difference. Personally, I'm looking forward to what's next."

Micky ends our session. "What a way to start a career. I bet we come up with ideas that'll make heads turn."

All CLUES Categories

12

Pennies in Your Pocket

SKILL: Interpersonal interaction

TOOL: Pennies transfer

CLUES CATEGORIES: Characteristics, Language, Underlying Motives, Energy, Stories

*P*eople are often promoted because of their technical expertise. When they reach the senior managerial ranks, however, their work emphasis switches from technical competence to competence with people—a role for which they are usually unprepared. With little support, they flounder in unfamiliar territory, feeling like imposters, fearful that their lack of interpersonal skills will be discovered.

This story illustrates how one such manager used the Pennies Transfer tool to gain awareness of his behavior and improve his interactions with employees.

THE SITUATION

A large manufacturing company begins a 360° feedback initiative that involves all senior executives. The most senior people are provided with individual coaches who will help them understand the feedback results and coach them on leadership.

I am assigned to Leo, executive vice-president of R&D. As I read his feedback report, I wonder how he has gotten so far in the organization. The majority of the 40 or so leadership practices show huge gaps between expectation and execution. In fact, this is the most negative report I've ever analyzed.

As Leo comes into the room for our initial meeting, his tie is askew, his shirt half out of his slacks, and his hair standing up in three directions. He pulls out his copy of the report and says, "I must be making 6,000 people miserable every day. So, how do we fix this?" I'm impressed with his candor and amused by his perception that these problems can easily be mended.

I ask Leo for his work history. His story is unsettlingly familiar: undergraduate and graduate degrees from first-rate engineering and science universities, internship in the space program, recruitment by private industry as a research fellow, promotion every two years or so in the technology arena. He joined R&D eight years ago and was appointed EVP three years ago.

Leo says that he's never had a formal performance review although he was reviewed on specific programs that he led (budget, delivery, quality, technological advances). When I ask him if he's taken any management training, he says that one summer he attended graduate school to learn project management. He does not remember if the course included people management.

When I inquire about his personal life, Leo tells me that he has been married to Bev for 22 years. She doesn't work outside the home although she is an active community volunteer. They have two children: Ron, 18, and Dorothy, 15.

In response to Leo's query about how to fix his problem, I explain, "Behaviors accumulate over time. I have no idea what you do to cause such strong reactions. I propose that I spend time as a fly on the wall to observe your specific behaviors. Then I'll be better equipped to give you ideas about how to approach your challenges."

The first event of observation day is a meeting with Leo's direct reports. He walks into the meeting, greets everyone with a general "hello," and tells them that I'm his coach. He says only that I'll be following him around for a few days. Next, Leo

picks out a chair, turns it away from the group seated around the table, and sits down with his back to them. During the meeting he shoots questions at the participants like a ball machine cranked up to the pro level. At the end of the meeting he thanks everyone but makes eye contact with only two people, both senior execs who seem similar to Leo in age, tenure, and academic background.

After the meeting I ask: "How come you sit with your back to people?" His reply is almost comical: "Because I don't want to be influenced by the way people look when they're talking. I just want to hear what they're talking about. That way I can react to ideas without getting caught up in 'who said what and why.'"

"Have you ever told that to your direct reports?" I ask.

Leo reacts: "No. Why would that matter? We're at a business meeting, not a knitting circle!"

I continue observing him. During the morning I write down action after action that frightens, disturbs, or angers employees. I watch people argue with Leo, turn red in the face, shut down, sigh (a lot), walk out of meetings shaking their head, swear under their breath, roll their eyes, and look vacant. At midday I decide to stop writing down the list of offending actions. The information I'm gathering will only fall on ears ill prepared to understand their meaning. I don't want to overwhelm Leo, either. As we move through the day, it becomes obvious to me that he is a very shy, introverted person with a vast store of technical knowledge. He has little ability to deal with people. At the end of the day I tell him, "I'll be back tomorrow with some thoughts." Leo doesn't even look up to say goodbye.

THE APPROACH

During the evening I mull over the day's events. I am reminded of Maslow's four-part hierarchy of consciousness:

1   Unconscious incompetence (being unaware that something is lacking).
2   Conscious incompetence (awareness of the lack).
3   Conscious competence (working to become competent in a new behavior).
4   Unconscious competence (performing consistently at a high level without effort).

Until Leo received the feedback report, he was in unconscious incompetence about his interpersonal skills because he was unaware that a problem existed. The report and my meeting with him should bring him into conscious incompetence. He will know that he's got a big problem. However, I'm not sure that he'll be able to identify what he does and says that creates such a wedge between him and others.

I decide that my goal is to raise Leo's level of awareness about his interactions with people. I want him to become fully conscious of his incompetence. It's pointless to give him a laundry list of dos and don'ts (do look at people when you talk to them, don't cut people off before they complete a sentence). Leo's fundamental problem of interacting with people manifests itself in hundreds of ways. He has to figure out what to say and do to be consciously competent, and there is no simple formula for that problem.

The following morning I discuss with Leo what I observed the previous day and explain Maslow's theory. I ask him, "Are you willing to conduct an experiment about the way you interact with others? It might help you to become more competent in that arena."

"Depends on the experiment," he retorts without changing his expression.

"Well, I've devised an experiment I'm calling Pennies Transfer." I reply. "Your job is to go to work every morning with ten pennies in your left-hand pocket and leave at night with ten pennies in your right-hand pocket. The only way to transfer a penny is to make a positive connection with another person."

"Like what?" Leo wants to know.

I suggest some ideas. "You can give someone a compliment like 'nice shoes' (he smiles at that) or 'good morning.' You

could place your chair to face people in the room. You could say, 'Thank you for that clear and cogent argument.'"

Looking worried, Leo says, "I got your drift. I'm willing to give it a try, just don't expect miracles."

"There's another component to this exercise," I tell him. "For you to learn from your successes as well as missteps, you've got to be conscious about what you're doing. Therefore, I'd like you to keep a journal of your thoughts and actions. I'd like you to pay attention to how others respond."

Leo quickly reacts, "No way. I'm not writing down everything I think and do. I hate to write—it takes too long."

I negotiate. "How about using a mini-tape recorder?"

"OK, I'll tape myself for one week. Then I'll overnight the tapes to you for your listening pleasure." (This is the first moment of levity we've shared.) We agree that he'll send me a tape for each day.

THE APPLICATION

From Day 1 tape: "I see Larry Ferguson pulling up in the parking garage. He'd be good to experiment with. He's an excellent scientist and almost as iconoclastic as I am. OK, I'm getting out of my car and shutting off this damn tape machine while I head over to where Larry's parked."

The tape resumes, apparently after Leo and Larry's interaction. "Well, I said 'good morning' to Larry, and he said the same to me. The only thing I could think of to talk to him about was the Stellar project he's been working on for a year. I don't know if that interaction deserves a penny switch. Marian told me to be lenient with myself at first, so I'll count it. I did notice Larry smiled when I came over to his car."

From Day 2 tape: "Margaret Nielson just left my office. I saw her at an operations review meeting yesterday where she asked for 30 minutes of my time. I told her to call Ginnie for my first available slot of time. It turns out that Margaret is going to head the Women's Council next year and she's concerned about how that will be perceived by the business unit. I asked why she's taking on such a politically sensitive extra job. Boy, the minute I asked that question, I saw pain in her face (I'm proud I recognized feelings by her facial expression). So, I fingered one of the pennies, looked straight at her, invited her to sit down, and asked the question in another—better—way. We spent the half hour talking about the Council, problems for women in my shop, and Margaret's and my role in working on the issue. Margaret thanked me for my support! I get a whole bunch of pennies switched for that one. And I actually enjoyed the conversation."

From Day 3 tape: "Damn, I really blew an opportunity. I'm on the company plane for a short trip with Ed, Frank, Marv, and Pat (what would happen to the company if the plane went down with half of the executive committee on it?). Anyhow, Marv suggested a solution to an ongoing, risky, very expensive problem. No sooner were the words out of his mouth than I began to hammer him with questions. I wanted to challenge his thinking. I always find it helpful to be questioned as part of the problem-solving process.

"But Marv looked at me with frustration and said, 'Leo, I don't need your negativity right now.' Since none of us handles conflict very well, we all fell silent. Fortunately Ed, being the capable CEO he is, soon chimed in and suggested that we talk about Marv's idea, each from our own knowledge and expertise. I felt like I reversed pennies on that one. Arguing about ideas is never personal for me. I guess not everyone feels the same way. But if we can't exchange opinions, we're doomed to end up with the same old stuff."

From Day 4 tape: "Here comes the test. I'm going into a meeting with my direct reports. Funny, Ginnie told me that a couple of people asked her what's up with the tape recorder and me. I guess I should say something. I decide to tell the group that I'm going to leave the tape recorder running during the meeting. I wonder what they'll say."

"Hello. Ginnie told me that you are curious about this tape recorder. I'm using it to keep a voice journal to share with my coach. I'm going to let it run for the first 15 minutes of the meeting." (Long pause and silence.)

"What's the problem?" Leo asks.

A voice: "Leo, it makes me uncomfortable to be taped. We talk about very sensitive issues here and I don't think it's appropriate to be taping our conversations, no matter how you intend to use them."

Another voice: "I think it's great you have a coach. I'd even be glad to pay for her or him. But I'm not interested in being a part of your assignment."

And another voice: "What would you get from taping this meeting anyway? How come you didn't ask us about the recorder being on?"

Leo: "Hmmm. These are legitimate questions. I thought taping the meeting would help Marian, my coach, and me understand what I do that causes reactions in people."

A voice: "Jeez Leo, if you want to know that, I'll give you an earful. I'm fireproof, so I'm not worried about what I say. You're the smartest scientist I know. I'll give you that. You've got a very good business head, too. But you're no picnic to work for. Is that enough?"

Leo: "How come no one ever said that to me before? What do I do that makes me so difficult?"

The first voice: "Leo, we're not shrinks here. Just be nicer to people, us included. For starters, smile once in a while and say, 'Thank you.'"

A new voice: "Now turn off that tape recorder and let's get down to business." (Silence.)

Leo: "Wow, that was some meeting! No one ever said a word to me about how I act before. The pennies feel like fingers in the dike: Move one and the water flows. I did do a few things differently at the meeting. I sat facing everyone, I looked at people when they spoke, and I tried like crazy not to interrupt."

From Day 5 tape: "I'm so glad it's Friday. This interpersonal stuff is exhausting. My son, Ron, thinks it's bogus (his term). He said I should just accept the fact that I'm not the best with people and let others who are handle that. I was hired to be the head of a research organization, not a schoolteacher.

"When I asked Ron how our communication is, he said, 'We

get along fine even though we don't talk about much besides science. I don't need you to be my pal, Dad. Dorothy might have a different story though.' Frankly, Dorothy is an enigma to me. I let her mother do the talking with her.

"I moved three pennies today. One was for telling Marv that his analysis of the Glenco deal was on target and very innovative. Marv looked at me with surprise and said that he appreciated my comments.

"Another was for telling Ginnie that I would not keep changing my calendar once she set it up. I can understand that it makes her look inefficient when she tells people that I am or am not available, and then I contradict her.

"Finally, I told three people I liked their shoes. [Laughter.] And I sent an email thanking my direct reports for their candid remarks about me. I said that they are good thinkers."

After I review the tapes from week I, Leo and I talk.

"Marian, how long will it take to feel natural with this stuff? Hard science is far easier than the pennies assignment. The most pennies I transferred in one day were three."

I ask, "How did those three people react?"

"Mostly, I don't think they trust me to change. They looked at me kind of funny, like I was acting. I realize now how distant I am with people. When you explained that I might act gruff because I'm shy, it made a lot of sense to me. My wife even has to pull me out of the house to go to parties. But I do love being at home with her and my kids, although she says I don't compliment any of them enough. She said I should put silver dollars in my pocket!"

The next week I shadow Leo once again to give him feedback on his progress. I notice how hard he's trying. The more he interacts, the more people talk to him. Even his appearance is neater. I tell him, "Your progress is being noted and appreciated by everyone you interact with."

"Look, Marian," he said, "I can see that this pennies trick is working, but I'm still uncomfortable. I don't like meetings. I dread getting stuck in the elevator with employees. I'm more exhausted than ever at the end of the day. I'm not sure the effort is worth the results."

I respond, "Leo, you've spent ten days trying on new behaviors to replace ones that you've grown accustomed to for over forty years. That's a huge challenge. Do you want to stop?"

"Nah, I don't want to go backwards," he says. "I don't like to diet, either; I just want the weight to be gone. If the pennies experiment were easy, I wouldn't need it. I'll keep going for one month, and then I'll let you know if I've changed my behavior or if this is a failed experiment. I'd like to continue sending you my tape journal and talking every week about what I've tried. I'd like suggestions from you. I guess everyone needs positive reinforcement."

THE RESULTS

At the end of the month my doorbell rings. It's a delivery from the florist. In the box with a dozen red roses there's a note that says, "I'm ready for a nickel. Thanks, Leo."

About six months later I return to shadow Leo for a follow-up day. One of his direct reports remarks to me in front of him, "You should patent and market whatever it is you brewed up for Leo. What a difference in his interactions with us! It's so much easier to work with him. What did you do?"

I responded, "I did little but give Leo support and a tool. He figured out how to use it. He did all the labor."

Part II

The Toolkit:

A User's Guide for Applying the
Five Coaching CLUES

Index Card System

PURPOSE

To provide a system that will help people who find it difficult to speak up at meetings gradually gain enough confidence and comfort to become regular contributors on the spot.

PROCESS

1 Take index cards of different colors into all the meetings you attend.

2 Once in a meeting, follow this scheme for writing down your questions, thoughts, and opinions:
   - ❑ *Blue* cards are for questions. For example: "What are the steps to the process you are introducing?" "How will you measure the success of this project?"
   - ❑ *Pink* cards are for ideas. For example: "Could you use the ABC study conducted last year to provide you with information on the subject?" "I know Hector in Chile is interested in the topic. Let's consult him."
   - ❑ *Yellow* cards are for opinions. For example: "I'm concerned that the timeline proposed is unrealistic." "I'd be very proud to be a part of this team because the work will have important and far-reaching results."

3 Whenever someone is talking and you have a question, idea, or opinion, write it on one of the cards. *Note*: It might be a good idea to forewarn people that this is a new work tool you're trying out, so they understand what you're doing and won't think you're writing comments about them.

4 When asked, read aloud what you've written on the cards. Often when people see you writing something down they'll be just plain curious; if someone asks you what you've written, read it out word for word.

5 If no one brings up your questions, ideas, or opinions, pick up the card and read it to the group. You need not explain what you're doing—let the card speak for you.

6 If it's too uncomfortable for you to read the card aloud you might ask someone to read it for you or give the cards to the appropriate person after the meeting. Note: If the meeting is not conducted in your first language, write the card in your native language and translate it later.

7 Once you're at ease using the cards, set a new goal for yourself. For example, you might decide that you will write at least one card of each color at a meeting, or that you will read every card out loud, or that you will give everyone who attended the meeting a copy of the cards you wrote.

8 Don't punish yourself if you fail to meet your own goals. Instead, reward yourself when you achieve what you set out to do—regardless of how small the goal. It might take quite a time to feel comfortable speaking up at meetings. Use the cards as long as they provide you with a reliable and easy-to-use aid.

Spring Cleaning Day

PURPOSE

To make the workplace more efficient by clearing areas of impediments that reduce productivity.

PROCESS

1 As an individual or a group who share a common workspace, tour the space and make a list of the objects in it.

2 Determine which of these objects may represent distractions: piles of work in disarray, for example, broken or marred knick-knacks or art pieces, books and magazines lying around, an overabundance of photos and memorabilia, too much or too little furniture to meet the needs of whoever works in the space, and, of course, simple trash. Hint: Write your list as though you were just taking inventory, without adding words of judgment: e.g., 14 file folders on floor, 9 photos of cats, 2 chipped glass vases. This can not only be fun, it can be a real eye-opener.

3 Set aside an uninterrupted period of time to deal with the items on your list and secure the approval of whichever level of management is relevant. This effort *must* be endorsed by the organization. Whether this is an individual or a group effort, spring cleaners are to have no other obligations during the designated time period and it must be clear that they will not be expected to make up the time spent on this task. In other words, Spring Cleaning Day is a working day.

4 Take photos of the space in question before, during, and after Spring Cleaning Day to show (yourself as well as others) what

you have accomplished. I find that not only do people like to get together to share what they've done, they also learn from one another about what they can do to enhance their working space.

5   It's a good idea to conduct a tour after the event to bask in the feeling of accomplishment and to acknowledge the help of anyone who has contributed to the effort.

6   Put another Spring Cleaning Day on the calendar as far in advance as seems reasonable, given what you've learned about your own habits or those of all the people in the group. (In my experience virtually every workspace can use a major tune-up from time to time.)

Inquiry Role-Play

PURPOSE
: To increase true dialogue in interactions by balancing advocacy—defending a position—with inquiry, that is, exploring for deeper understanding.

PROCESS

1 Write up a brief case study that reflects a common dilemma in your organization. The following is an example:

   Charles and his wife recently had a baby. When Charles returns from paternity leave, he informs his department that he will no longer work past 5.30 p.m. nor on weekends. His co-worker Mary Beth is single. Within a week of Charles's announcement, Mary Beth realizes that she is now getting the overflow work that Charles cannot cope with because of his reduced hours. Mary Beth goes to their manager to discuss the issues of single versus family people and the distribution of work.

2 Convene the group of people you're hoping to train in this new skill—you need enough people so that each can take the role of one of the players in your hypothetical dilemma; ideally, the group would be large enough so that there can be two such teams. For best results, you'll also need a tape recorder. There are four rounds to the role-play itself:

Round 1

❑ Divide the participants into role-playing teams; for the example above that would be trios.
❑ Assign roles to the members of each group (e.g., Charles, Mary Beth, and the manager).

❑ Tell the teams they have 10 minutes to work on the situation. Each person is to stay in his or her assigned role for the entire time.

❑ Tape-record the interaction.

❑ Ask the teams to listen to the tape of their interaction.

❑ On paper, have each team member note when they hear themselves advocating for a particular position (e.g., "Having a new baby requires a lot of time and attention that I used to give to work"). Also have each team member note when they hear themselves inquiring about what someone else is saying, thinking, or feeling (e.g., "Charles, what are the implications of your new hours for the rest of the department?").

After Round 2, explain what inquiry and advocacy are and the reasons both are necessary for effective communication and problem solving:

Advocacy is defending a position. Advocacy is appropriate when opinions and desires can be well articulated and supported, especially during the final decision-making process.

Inquiry is exploring for understanding. Inquiry is especially appropriate in the early stages of coming to grips with a situation, particularly when there is a lack of clarity or when people are making unexamined assumptions in advocating one course of action over another.

Too much advocacy can result in overly swift decision making that does not reflect the thinking of all parties involved in or affected by the decision. Endless inquiry, however, can result in paralysis.

My experience in coaching, especially with problem-solving groups, is that advocacy is the norm and inquiry is rare. Yet when people learn how to increase their practice of inquiry, the quality of the decisions that result goes up dramatically. I believe that the advocacy-prone phenomenon comes from the fact that most people in most organizations assume that they

Round 2

Advocacy

Inquiry

are responsible for knowing the answer even before they truly understand the question.

Round 3

❑ Put all of the people playing a given role together, forming the same number of new teams as there are roles in the dilemma. In the example, there would be a team of Mary Beths, of Charleses, and of managers.

❑ Ask these new, same-character teams to develop a series of inquiries that they can ask the players of the other roles (e.g., what can Mary Beth ask Charles and/or the manager?).

Round 4

❑ Reconvene the original teams and resume the role-play.

❑ Ask the teams to try to achieve a better balance between advocacy and inquiry by using the inquiry questions developed in Round 3.

❑ After the role-play is completed, ask the trios about the differences between this round and the first, tape-recorded round.

❑ Capture and discuss their insights.

Note: This exercise needs a leader. Every time I work with an individual or a group that is focusing on improving and increasing their habit of inquiry, I ask for feedback about what they are noticing, examples of good inquiry they used or heard, and comments about the impact of increased inquiry on the quality of their communication and decision making. The leader becomes the placeholder for more inquiry until it has become second nature for the other participants.

Another note: If you're conducting this role-play with only one other person, follow the same process but modify it accordingly (e.g., you play a role in the dilemma; have the person write questions for him- or herself in Round 3).

Listening Loop

To prevent expensive mistakes caused by action taken without clarity about the content and/or intent of what is said in a presentation.

1 After a speech or presentation (formal or informal), participants write down all of the points that they recall the presenter making.

2 Each point is written on a separate sticky note (3"×5" or 4"×6", to provide a writing surface large enough for others to read).

3 Post the notes.

4 Put the notes into categories and label the categories.

5 The speaker uses colored markers or sticky dots to indicate his or her reaction to the notes:
   - ❑ Green indicates agreement (yes, that's what I meant).
   - ❑ Orange calls for clarification.
   - ❑ Red sounds the alarm of disagreement.

6 *Green* notes require no further discussion. I find that far too much time is spent talking about points of agreement. Use your time on the orange and red notes.

7 *Orange* notes require interaction. The participants need to ask clarifying questions of the speaker. They should be

careful not to challenge the speaker; rather, they should inquire in a reasonable way about points that might have different interpretations, connotations, and meanings, or might contain information of which they were not aware.

8   *Red* notes require skillful probing to get at the basis for the disagreement. If the speaker and the other participants have widely diverging views on a topic, they might have to agree to disagree and put this item on a "parking lot" list for further examination.

9   After all of the items on all three of the lists have been discussed, the speaker reiterates the points on the orange and red lists and determines, with the participants, which items have moved to green. *Note:* It is very important to leave with a clear understanding of which points now belong on the list of agreements (green) and which are still the subject of disagreements (the red list). There should be no orange items outstanding.

10 If there is a parking lot, that too requires further action, which must be decided on before adjourning.

11 At the conclusion of the Listening Loop, or shortly thereafter, a summary of the points and their final designated color (green or red) should be distributed to the attendees.

Time Use Matrix

Formal meetings							
Activities							
Objectives	NMI Team	Cross-functional projects	Universal Charity Fund	Summer Family Sports Program	Weekly departmental status meeting	Bi-weekly meeting with boss	Rotating performance reviews
A Increase market share	1, 2, 3, 4, 5, 6						
B Develop direct reports	7						
C Build cross-functional systems	1, 3, 5						
D Position self for VP slot	1, 2, 5, 6						
E Establish information networks	1, 3, 4, 5						

Criteria: 1 Meets objective; 2 Personal enjoyment; 3 Learning opportunity; 4 Immediate application; 5 Long-term payoff; 6 Cannot be delegated; 7 Not applicable

PURPOSE

To ascertain the impact and value of the way in which time is used and make changes to increase productivity.

PROCESS

1 List your key job objectives. Write them in alphabetical order in the left-hand column of a matrix like the one overleaf.

2 Use your calendar or daily log to identify the activities that you undertake in a work day or work week. Write these across the top of the matrix.

3 Develop some criteria for judging the importance of your activities. (For example, if you're new in a job, one criterion might be how the activity helps you "learn the ropes" and climb the learning curve.) Five to seven criteria are a reasonable number to handle at once. Number the criteria and write them along the bottom of the matrix. (I've provided three common ones at the bottom of the matrix overleaf.)

4 In each cell where your objectives and activities intersect, write the number(s) of the criteria that are satisfied. (In our example, it appears that holding weekly staff meetings is a valuable activity for developing staff because it meets several of the criteria listed.)

5 After the entire matrix is complete, revisit it to review your entries.

Objectives	Activities						
	Hold weekly staff meetings						
A Develop staff	1, 2, 3						
B							
C							
D							
E							

Criteria: 1 Within my control; 2 Long-term value; 3 Short-term solution, etc.

6   Highlight in green the activities with the highest value and in red the activities with the least value.

7   Reconfigure the matrix to assign the ideal amount of time to spend on each of your current activities. Don't be afraid to redline some of them.

8   Develop a plan to implement your new time use analysis.

9   Share your plan and tell people exactly what you will be doing differently and why. For example, you might decide that in the future you won't take any phone calls or be available for office visits between 8 and 9 a.m. because that time will be spent assessing the delivery schedule of each project in the department.

10 Periodically review and change the matrix as workloads and tasks shift. The intent is for the matrix to be a working document that allows you to be in charge of your day and helps you become more productive.

The Beginner's Mind

PURPOSE

To make change in a process or habit of thinking by returning to a state of mind we all possessed at a time when everything was new, before training, experience, and prior judgments—as invaluable as they often are—dictated our first-line approach to how things should be done.

PROCESS

1 Define the problem. For example, there might be a way of doing a particular task—large or small—in a given company that no one dares question despite the fact that it may not add value to either the company's functioning or its products, but rather the reverse.

2 Trace the origin of the issue. Ask first of all and repeatedly, "What is this supposed to accomplish?" Be persistent. Once you find out when and why a particular practice was begun and for what purpose, you'll be better able to decide whether it's still useful or not and/or to make suggestions about modifying it.

3 Design an experiment to determine what it's like to experience the process as a "customer," not its "owner." (For example, let's say the problem is that people complain about registering for professional development classes. Put yourself in their shoes and go through every step, keeping a log of every thought and frustration, hitch and help.)

4   Ask at every juncture, "Must it be this way? What else could work?" Write down all your ideas, no matter how fleeting.

5   Revise the process to include your new ideas.

6   Monitor the new process until it works to the satisfaction of those "customers" who complained in the first place.

Delegation Triangle Checklist

WILL DO
• Will
• Incentive
• Nurturing

TO DO
• Complexity
• Length
• Expectations
• Availability
• Resources

DELEGATION

CAN DO
• Skills
• Experience
• Training

PURPOSE

To diagnose the degree to which people are prepared to give and receive a delegated task, and to help managers learn when and to whom to delegate responsibility.

PROCESS

1   Before meeting with the person to whom you want to delegate, fill in the Delegation Triangle Checklist (overleaf) based on your knowledge of the person and the situation. This action is to focus your thinking; it is not intended to control the conversation or the outcome of the meeting.

2   Bring the checklist to the delegation meeting. You might also want to send a copy to the potential delegatee before your face-to-face meeting to reduce anxiety and facilitate the interaction.

3   Talk with the delegatee and go over each of the points on the checklist. Do not assume that any of your Step 1 responses will be echoed by the delegatee. *Note*: You may have to ask some probing questions to clarify a response or get beyond short or incomplete answers. Never ask, "Do you understand?" Most often the delegatee will say yes because he or she doesn't want to appear inadequate. Instead you could ask, "Explain to me your understanding of the task."

4 At the end of the meeting, review the checklist and confirm what you've both agreed to, then establish the next action steps.

THE DELEGATION TRIANGLE CHECKLIST

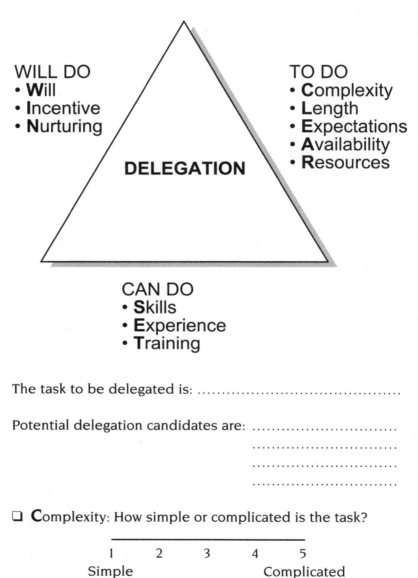

WILL DO
- **W**ill
- **I**ncentive
- **N**urturing

TO DO
- **C**omplexity
- **L**ength
- **E**xpectations
- **A**vailability
- **R**esources

DELEGATION

CAN DO
- **S**kills
- **E**xperience
- **T**raining

The task to be delegated is: ....

Potential delegation candidates are: ....
....
....
....

TO DO

❑ **C**omplexity: How simple or complicated is the task?

1	2	3	4	5
Simple				Complicated

❑ **L**ength: How long will the task take to complete?

#Days: ....
#Weeks: ....
#Months: ....

❑ **E**xpectations: What are my (the delegator's) expectations?

My expectations:
1
2
3

What are your (the delegatee's) expectations?

His/her expectations:
1
2
3

❑ **A**vailability: When am I, the delegator, available to coach?

Times available	Monday	Tuesday	Wednesday	Thursday	Friday

When is the delegatee available to be coached?

Times available	Monday	Tuesday	Wednesday	Thursday	Friday

❏ **R**esources: Are there appropriate resources to support the delegatee?

Resources available:
1
2
3

WILL DO

❏ **W**ill: Does the delegatee have the desire, curiosity, fortitude, and commitment to do what is necessary to accomplish the task?

Desire: Yes ❏ No ❏   Don't know ❏

Curiosity: Yes ❏ No ❏   Don't know ❏

Fortitude: Yes ❏ No ❏   Don't know ❏

Commitment: Yes ❏ No ❏   Don't know ❏

❏ **I**ncentive: What's in it for the delegatee?

Possible incentives:
❏   Learning
❏   Job advancement
❏   Money
❏   Time
❏   Exposure
❏
❏

❏ **N**urturing: Will the delegatee feel secure enough to take on a risk?

Security factors: Yes ❏ No ❏   Don't know ❏

❑ **S**kills: Does the delegatee have the technical and personal skills to accomplish the task?

CAN DO

Technical skills: Yes ❑ No ❑   Don't know ❑

Personal skills: Yes ❑ No ❑   Don't know ❑

❑ **E**xperience: Does the delegatee have the prior experience to accomplish the task?

Prior experience: Yes ❑ No ❑   Don't know ❑

❑ **T**raining: Does the delegatee have access to any training necessary to accomplish the task?

Potential training access:
❑	On-the-job training	Yes ❑	No ❑	Don't know ❑
❑	Classroom	Yes ❑	No ❑	Don't know ❑
❑	E-learning	Yes ❑	No ❑	Don't know ❑
❑	Web-based	Yes ❑	No ❑	Don't know ❑
❑	Mentor	Yes ❑	No ❑	Don't know ❑
❑	College/tech school	Yes ❑	No ❑	Don't know ❑
❑				
❑				

"Write, Speak, Post" Brainstorming

PURPOSE
To build on established brainstorming methods and guidelines to accommodate a wide range of thinking styles and cultural differences.

PROCESS

1 Develop a statement to identify the topic for brainstorming clearly, then convene your team. For example, a clear statement is "What beauty items might teens purchase?" or "What might the causes be for an employee turnover rate of 72%?"

2 Give everyone pads of large (3"×5" or 4"×6") sticky notes (the usual small ones aren't adequate for these purposes and will just drive everyone crazy) and prepare a space—a conference-sized paper pad on an easel, a section of black-, green-, or white-board, or just a big part of the wall—to receive those notes.

3 Ask brainstormers to write down their ideas about the topic, one idea at a time per sticky note.

4 As soon as anyone writes the idea down, he or she says it out loud so everyone can hear it.

5 After the idea is spoken, the brainstormer hands it off to a facilitator to post on the wall or easel. If there is no facilitator, the participants post their own ideas.

Note for the facilitator: When an idea is handed to you, say thank you. Throughout the posting process make encouraging but non-evaluative remarks, along the lines of "You're coming up with a lot of ideas," or "It's great to see you working so hard," or "Wow, you're filling the entire wall," or "Everyone's contributing." Never exhort the group to produce and never say anything negative.

6   If you sense that the group is running out of steam, ask them to stretch by playing around "off the clock." For example, you might ask them what were the riskiest ideas that crossed their minds, the ones they thought were too "far out" to post. And take note of any, no matter how wild, that seem promising.

7   Keep the timeframe flexible and avoid a deadline mentality. Deadlines can be stimulating, but all too often they put too much pressure on the group and inhibit rather than encourage creativity.

8   Thank everyone for their ideas and take a well-deserved break before asking people to return and evaluate them.

You might also ask what it was like to use this tool. People are often flabbergasted by the number of ideas they generate if given the right circumstances. In particular, introverts and people who are not native English speakers seem to respond to the opportunity this exercise offers them to contribute at their own pace and in their own fashion.

Visual Essay and Metaphorical Thinking

PURPOSE

To reframe a problem or situation by taking a mental excursion to look at it from a new and different perspective.

PROCESS

1 Write a clear, brief problem statement. Note: See the Storytelling tool (page 159) for guidance on writing problem statements.

2 Divide the group into smaller subgroups of four to six people at most. You can do this in a planned or arbitrary way. For example, you can count off by fours or divide the room into birthday quartiles, or preassign people so that various parts of the organization will be represented in each group.

3 Based on the problem statement, identify or create at least as many components as there are small groups. (Let's say the problem statement is "How might we reconnect with previous customers?" and there are twenty people in the large group, which you've divided into four smaller ones. To accommodate each group you might create four or more different categories of "previous customers.") Write each component on a slip of paper and put them in a bowl or a box or the proverbial hat.

4 Ask each team to appoint an emissary to select the component (customer category in our example) on which they'll work. Note: I usually have more components than groups just to make sure that the last group to pick doesn't feel they got stuck with a leftover.

5 Each emissary pulls a slip of paper out of the "hat." (In the example cited above it would represent one of the four or more customer categories.)

6 Hand out copies of the following instruction sheet—modified to fit the problem statement components you've devised—to each team. (The version below reflects our "previous customer" example.)

Instructions:

❑ At 1 p.m. tomorrow you will present a visual essay about the group identified on the card you selected.
❑ The essay is to tell a story about that group and how its members use our products/services.
❑ Your presentation may not exceed 15 minutes.
❑ To complete this assignment you may choose a video or disposable camera; collage made from magazines, newspapers, journals, or company printed materials; objects found in nature; or any combination of the above.
❑ Develop a central metaphor for the essay. (A metaphor uses analogy to represent some salient characteristic of the person or object or action.) You might begin your metaphor with "This category reminds me of ...." or "These customers are like ...."

7 As the presentations are given, write the messages gleaned from each group's offerings—both the visual essays and the metaphors—on large sheets of paper posted on the wall or mounted on an easel. Each visual essay generates its own list.

8 Compare the lists and look for themes and patterns. Some themes will be specific to a particular problem component and others will cross all categories.

9 Ask: "What can we take from these lists to regain previous customers as clients?" Capture those ideas.

10 Begin the converging process by combining like ideas, and put these idea clusters into priority order. *Note*: You

might want to establish criteria to guide the prioritization process.

11 Assign responsibility for developing the highest-priority ideas and putting them into practice.

Note: You might also want to post the visual essays in whatever serves as your company bulletin board and ask for ideas from others in the organization.

Talking Stick

PURPOSE

To govern the process that a group employs to share information and ideas by using a ceremonial symbol.

PROCESS

1 Select a stick from the forest, or a park, or your yard—the point is that it's an object found in nature—and decorate one end of it (with paint, feathers, hide, beads, etc.) to make it beautiful and personal, leaving a space large enough to accommodate a hand. Let the other end remain unadorned.

2 Bring the talking stick to a meeting and explain its significance as a symbol—one that is to be shared—of the speaker who has the floor.

3 Sit in a circle.

4 Place the stick in the center of the circle.

5 When you're ready to begin talking, pick up the stick. The decorated end is held and the undecorated end is pointed toward the center of the circle.

6 Speak until you have said what you want to say. There are to be no interruptions of the speaker.

7 When you have finished talking, offer the talking stick to the group by turning it around so the decorated end is ready for another person to grasp.

8 The next speaker takes the decorated end and begins to talk. It's not necessary to go in any order. Reach out to ask for the stick when you have something to add.

9 Continue the process until everyone has spoken at least once.

10 To signal the end of the dialogue the talking stick is once again placed in the center of the circle. Wait a few moments before adjourning to allow everyone to ponder what has been said.

Note: I'm often asked, "But how do you make sure one person doesn't just hang on to the stick and monopolize the discussion?" In fact, because the talking stick focuses people's attention on the group's acknowledgment of the speaker's right to be heard without interruption, they tend to become quite sensitive about the need to hear from all members of the group who have something to say, and they usually regulate their own behavior accordingly. That's the beauty of this tool.

Storytelling

PURPOSE

Increase the likelihood of solving a chronic or ill-defined problem by using the collective knowledge of people who have had experience with its parameters in the past.

PROCESS

Note: The Storytelling tool has many steps within steps, and it may sometimes be necessary to stretch the process out over several days. However, once you're familiar with it you can streamline the process by eliminating those steps that aren't relevant in a given situation and achieve results much more quickly, sometimes in the space of a single meeting.

1　Receive the partially cooked problem. Read or hear a summary of the situation as it is currently understood. Then convene an inclusive meeting for an opening discussion. Provide pens and large sticky notes for recording questions and answers, and offer a place to post them.

❑ Invite all (or at least a representative sample) of those who are currently affected by the problem or have had experience with it in the past (this might even include former employees).

❑ Ask clarifying questions but request that people keep their answers brief for now.

❑ Keep a record of questions and brief summaries of the answers you've heard.

❑ Put questions that can't be answered on a "parking lot" section of the wall.

2 Invite people to tell individual stories as briefly as they can. Each story will add to the cumulative body of knowledge about the problem or situation. Ask people to follow these guidelines:
   ❑ One person speaks at a time without any interruptions (remember the Talking Stick).
   ❑ Each person adds to what has previously been said without repeats.
   ❑ Begin your story with the word "and" (you're building an encyclopedia).
   ❑ It's not necessary to go in order; speak when your additions seem most appropriate.
   ❑ Talk about what you know: history, your involvement, experiences, people; the good, the bad, and the ugly.
   ❑ Speak your truth—only you know it.
   ❑ Everyone speaks at least once.

3 Identify key aspects of the problem.
   ❑ Divide into small groups to identify patterns and themes that have surfaced in the stories. For example, "Our equipment always lags behind the state of the art," or "We have smart people in our company and they are leaving," or "We make changes without talking about why we're changing," or "The such-and-such method we used eight years ago seems to have possibilities today."
   ❑ Write one pattern or theme per sticky note—use the felt pens distributed about the room. Then post your sticky notes on the paper-covered wall.
   ❑ After you're finished posting your work, walk around to read everyone's entries.

4 Combine aspects of the problem.
   ❑ Combine repeated ideas.
   ❑ Don't discard repeats, because later the number of repeats might indicate the relative importance of ideas.
   ❑ Then cluster like ideas together and give each cluster a title.

5 Write a series of problem statements to address different aspects of the situation as they have been revealed by the idea clusters.

❑ Write problem statements for each of the idea clusters identified. Writing a strong problem statement is the trickiest part of problem solving. If the problem statement doesn't invite innovative thinking, the best one can hope for is a Band-Aid solution.

❑ Develop criteria for evaluating the problem statements. The criteria will help focus what the problem statement should include.

❑ Sample criteria:
Is breakthrough thinking possible?
Will it be worthy of the resources that are to be spent?
Will the solving this aspect of the larger problem make a real difference?
Is there passion in the organization for doing so?
Can it be achieved?

❑ Use "How might we" (HMW) to begin the problem statements. This is a phrase that is invitational and open. For example, "How might we reduce attrition in middle-management ranks?'

6 Multi-vote to select the critical few aspects of the larger situation to be addressed first. In doing so, consider the criteria you've developed. Here's an outline of a multi-voting process:

❑ Total the number of problem statements.

❑ Divide that number by five, e.g., fifteen problem statements divided by five results is three votes per person.

❑ Give each person three votes, in the form of colored sticky dots to be placed on the problem statements.

❑ Ask each person to vote according to the established criteria. That is, which problem statement(s) best meet the criteria?

❑ Each voter can place all of his or her dots on one problem statement or spread them out among various statements.

❑ The problem statements with the greatest number of votes are addressed first.

Note: I find that people who get to choose which problem statement they want to work on are the most enthusiastic and come up with the best ideas.

Bring the process to an end only when you have clear problem statements, assignments for populating teams to address each one, and a schedule for taking the next steps.

Pennies Transfer

To change one's own behavior by using a physical reminder to reward success.

1 Identify the behavior on which you want to work. For example, giving more positive feedback to people, reducing the amount of time you spend chatting at the water cooler, or contributing more ideas in meetings.

2 Put ten pennies in the left pocket of your jacket or sweater, pants or skirt.

3 Move one penny to your right pocket every time you change/modify your behavior. For example, each time you give someone positive feedback, move a penny. ("That report you submitted is very well written and I learned a lot from it," for example, or "I appreciate your willingness to stay late and help me with the proposal." Or just a simple "Well done.")

4 Each day, note how many pennies you switched. Keep a record to track your progress. Repeat successful tactics. Be honest with yourself about what didn't work and reframe your approach if need be.

5 Talk with a few people about the behavior you are modifying. Ask them how they think it's working and what

suggestions they might be able to give you to help you improve even more.

6 Celebrate both small steps and big strides.

7 Continue the process until you've switched at least ten pennies every day for ten consecutive days. (Until then the new pattern of behavior is not ingrained in your subconscious. The goal is to make it a habit of which you're hardly aware.)

List of Skills

Index by Skills

COACHING FOR PERFORMANCE
GROWing People, Performance and Purpose
Third edition

JOHN WHITMORE

Clear, concise, hands-on and friendly, **Coaching for Performance** is a coaching guide written in a coaching style. This bestselling handbook will help you learn the skills—and the art—of good coaching, and realize its enormous value in unlocking people's potential to maximize their own performance. Adopted by many of the world's major corporations, this easy-to-use title argues persuasively for using questions rather than instructions or commands, and following the GROW sequence—**G**oals, **R**eality, **O**ptions, **W**ill—to generate prompt action and peak performance. This third edition of *the* definitive guide moves on to new psychological ground with three new chapters on coaching for personal meaning at work, purpose in goal-setting and the corporation's own culture—to **GROW People, Performance and Purpose** together.

Sir John Whitmore consults and lectures widely on human resource management together with his colleagues David Hemery and David Whitaker of *Performance Consultants*.

UK £12.99, US $17.95
Paperback 1 85788 303 9
194pp 234×189mm

COACHING ACROSS CULTURES
New Tools for Leveraging
National, Corporate, and Professional Differences

PHILIPPE ROSINSKI

As coaches and clients increasingly realize, the demands of business mean that it is now vital to integrate, understand, and leverage cultural differences across countries and corporations. This work bridges the gap between coaching and interculturalism. **Coaching Across Cultures** is the first book to join together the fields of executive, team, and personal coaching with cross-cultural communication. It is filled with intriguing examples from multinational companies, and includes coaching tools with exercises that put into practice the cultural concepts presented. This book will help you become aware of your own national and corporate cultural orientations and how they affect the way you coach.

Philippe Rosinski is an experienced professional coach who has worked with multinational corporations both in the US and Europe over the past decade. He was the first European to achieve the designation of Master Certified Coach by the International Coach Federation.

UK £19.99, US $29.95
Paperback 1 85788 301 2
338pp 234×156mm

NICHOLAS BREALEY PUBLISHING

new *books* new *business*

People Skills for Professionals Series

COACHING FOR PERFORMANCE
John Whitmore
UK £12.99, US $17.95 PB ISBN 1 85788 303 9

NLP AT WORK
Sue Knight
UK £14.99, US $19.95 PB ISBN 1 85788 302 0

INNER LEADERSHIP
Simon Smith
UK £12.99, US $17.95 PB ISBN 1 85788 271 7

THE POWER OF INFLUENCE
Tom Lambert
UK £12.99, US $17.95 PB ISBN 1 85788 115 X

LEADING YOUR TEAM
Andrew Leigh and Michael Maynard
UK £12.99, US $17.95 PB ISBN 1 85788 304 7

THE TRUST EFFECT
Larry Reynolds
UK £12.99, US $17.95 PB ISBN 1 85788 186 9

COACHING ACROSS CULTURES
Philippe Rosinski
UK £19.99, US $29.95 PB ISBN 1 85788 301 2

ORDER FORM

Title	ISBN	Price	Qty	Cost
Postage UK or surface mail outside the UK (replace with £8.00 for airmail)				+ £2.95
			TOTAL	

Titles are available from all good bookshops, OR
SEND YOUR COMPLETED ORDER TO: Nicholas Brealey Publishing

3–5 Spafield St
London EC1R 4QB
Tel: +44 (0)20 7239 0360
Fax: +44 (0)20 7329 0370

PO Box 700
Yarmouth, Maine 04096, USA
Tel: (888) BREALEY
Fax: (207) 846 5181

BY CHEQUE: I enclose a cheque (payable to Nicholas Brealey Publishing) for . . . .

BY CREDIT CARD: I authorize you to debit my credit card account for . . . .

My Mastercard/Visa/American Express/Diners Club card number is:

Expiry date: . . . . Tel no: . . . .

Cardholder's name: . . . . Signature: . . . .

Position: . . . . Organization: . . . .

Address: . . . . Postcode: . . . .